I0463535

Launch, Grow and Make Money!

Become a Home Inspector

Kirk Bingenheimer

2014 © Kirk Bingenheimer

All rights reserved

ISBN: 150069990X

ISBN-13: 978-1500699901

Dedication

This book is dedicated to my wife Mia Bingenheimer. Mia helped get my home inspection business of the ground. She was there to encourage me through the early days of not even knowing how I was going to get my first inspection to three years later when we were performing more than 400 inspections annually. Thank you honey!

TABLE OF CONTENTS

Introduction

Before You Start

Launch Your Business

Grow Your Business

Make Money Inspecting Homes

About The Author

Acknowledgments

Appendix

Introduction

Before I started my home inspection business, I worked in the construction education and the production home building industry for nearly twenty years. I spent three years teaching at Clemson University after obtaining my Masters in Building Science and Management in 1991. For the next fifteen years or so I worked for several large regional and national production home builders. In September of 2009 I launched my home inspection business in the Charleston, SC market.

I recall having a lunch meeting with my CPA about two weeks before I launched my new business. She asked me how I was going to obtain new clients. To be honest I actually had no idea! It was at that moment that my journey to obtain paying customers began. I felt confident about my ability to perform a home inspection. However, I did not have any idea what it would take to market myself and operate a professional home inspection service.

After a lot of hard work and many lessons learned my company performed more than 400 inspections annually in our third year of business. With a solid business model now in place I am ready to share my secrets of effective home inspection marketing and operational systems. The purpose of this book is to share with you my journey to launch, grow and make money inspecting residential properties. You will learn **what** it takes to be a successful home inspector. The first section of this book reviews what to consider before you start your business. Part two is about what you need to do to launch your new home inspection business. Part three is an overview of the strategies it takes to grow your inspection business. The final section looks at the systems you need to make money inspecting homes.

You have three choices to become a home inspector: start from scratch, purchase an existing business or purchase a franchise system. While the choice is yours, the hardest part is a commitment to just get started.

Kirk Bingenheimer

Before You Start

TM

Keep it Simple

Perhaps the hardest thing about owning and operating a home inspection business is to stay focused on your primary mission: perform thorough home inspections for people buying or selling houses. That is why I apply my Keep Inspection Systems Simple (KISS) principle every time I think about changing a process or adding additional inspection services. I challenge every home inspector to apply the KISS principle to their own business on a daily basis.

There are a variety of home inspection related products and services that want to take money out of your pocket. As you are exposed to these opportunities through blogs, websites, direct emails or attending a home inspection conferences you need to decide if these services really add any value to your business. Do not let other people give you the impression that you will not be a successful home inspector without purchasing their product or using their service. Apply the KISS principle to each home inspection related product or service you encounter.

As a member of the American Society of Home Inspectors (ASHI) I am required to obtain 20 hours of continuing education credits every year. One of the best ways to accomplish this is to attend home inspection conferences that provide classes for you to earn the continuing education credits required for membership. In addition to the classes you have a wonderful opportunity to network with other home inspectors from across the country. The conversations that you have with these inspectors can be just as valuable as what you learn from the instructors in the classes.

Another important part of most home inspection conferences is the vendor expo. Vendors set up booths outside the classrooms to display their home inspection products or services. At these shows you will see a variety of products and services to consider incorporating into your home inspection business. Some of these offerings have high value and others may not. As you look at each product or service learn as much as you can about it and do not make rash decisions on the spot. If there is something that you believe will add value to your home inspection business jot it down. Think about it for a week or two before you make a decision. Apply the KISS principle as you evaluate the possibility of incorporating this new product or service into your business. Remember that each change that you make to your home inspection systems or services may have a potential value <u>and</u> most certainly will add to the expense of operating your business.

Join a Professional Home Inspector Association

Before you begin your career as a home inspector you should research and join one of the leading home inspection associations. The major organizations that represent the home inspection industry are the American Society of Home Inspectors (ASHI), the National Association of Home Inspectors (NAHI) and the International Association of Certified Home Inspectors (InterNACHI).

The American Society of Home Inspectors [www.ashi.org] is the oldest and perhaps the most respected home inspection association. It was founded in 1976 by a group of visionary home inspectors with the common goal of building consumer awareness and to enhance the professionalism of their field. ASHI established standards of practice and a strict code of ethics for their member community. The mission of ASHI is to meet the needs of its membership and promote excellence and exemplary practice within the home inspection profession. The highest level of membership is the ASHI Certified Inspector (ACI). To become an ACI you must have completed at least 250 paid inspections, passed the ASHI code of ethics module and passed the National Home Inspectors Examination (NHIE). The NHIE [www.homeinspectionexam.org] is a proctored 200 question closed book exam.

The National Association of Home Inspectors [www.nahi.org] was established in 1987 to promote and develop certified and licensed home inspectors in the professional home inspection industry. NAHI focuses on education and developed standards of practice for the exclusive use by its members.

The International Association of Certified Home Inspectors is the world's largest home inspection association. InterNACHI [www.nachi.org] provides education, training, certification, benefits and support for its members. InterNACHI members follow a comprehensive standard of practice and abide by a strict code of ethics. They also require accredited continuing education courses each year and have their own home inspector certification examination.

There is no right or wrong home inspection association to belong to. The most important thing is that you join at least one of them and strictly follow their standards of practice and code of ethics. Each organization also requires a certain amount of continuing education classes each year in order to maintain membership. In many cases these continuing education credits can be earned by participating in local association meetings or attending their regional/national conferences. There are also several third-party organizations that offer continuing education for home inspectors as well.

Select a Limited Liability Entity

With any business you should attempt to limit your personal liabilities for the work you perform for your clients. Since home inspectors are typically preforming a limited visual examination of the properly, we should not be liable for every possible problem the home may have. If one of your clients claim that you missed something during the inspection you want to have some protection against your personal assets. In order to do this most home inspectors, set up a limited liability entity for their business. The most common small business structures are a sole proprietor, corporation and limited liability company.

The sole proprietorship is a type of business entity that is owned and run by one person and there is not a legal distinction between the owner and the owner's business. The owner earns profits and has unlimited liability and is responsible for any losses or debts. If something bad happens with the business the personal assets of the sole proprietor may be in jeopardy. A sole proprietor may use a business name that is different than their personal name. The advantages of are that they are easy to organize, have a high degree of flexibility and owner receives all of the profits. The disadvantages of this structure include limited ability to raise capital, unlimited liability for business debts and possible loss of personal property if the business fails and owes money to its debtors.

A corporation is a separate legal entity that has been established through state legislation. Corporations have legal rights and liabilities that are separate from their employees and shareholders. They tend to have limited liability and are owned by a shareholder who can transfer their shares to others. Corporations are controlled by a board of directors and they are normally elected or appointed by the corporation's shareholders. Corporations are usually registered through state governments and regulated by the laws enacted by the state. The corporation files articles of incorporation which outlines the general nature of the corporation, the amount of stock authorized for use along with the names and addresses of the board of directors.

Another option for home inspectors is to form a Limited Liability Company (LLC). A LLC is an entity that has certain characteristics of a corporation or sole proprietorship. The LLC is a legal form of a company that provides limited liability to its owners, known as members. It also has the ability to pass-through profits to the member owner(s) tax returns. This structure is more flexible than a corporation and is well-suited for companies that have a single owner. The LLC can elect to be taxed as a sole proprietor, s-corporation or a c-corporation.

The type of limited liability entity that you choose for your home inspection business depends on several factors. In contrast to the sole proprietorship, the corporation or the LLC provides you with some legal protection of your personal assets for the actions you take with your business. If you plan to have partners in the business the corporation may be beneficial but there is a good bit of regulation surrounding the operation of a corporation. The LLC by contrast is well suited for a single owner of the business. It doesn't limit your ambitions to grow the business (multi-inspector company) and the profits are transferred directly to your personal tax return. Be sure the consult with an attorney or tax consultant to choose the best form of legal protection for your home inspection business. A tax attorney or third-part entity such as Legal Zoom can walk you through the process of creating your corporate or LLC documents.

Obtain Your Employer Identification Number

If you choose a Corporation or Limited Liability Company you will need a Federal Employer Identification Number (EIN) for your home inspection business. This number is the corporate equivalent to a personal Social Security number. This number is issued to either individuals, corporations or limited liability companies for the purpose of withholding Federal taxes. The EIN is a unique nine-digit number assigned by the Internal Revenue Service (IRS) to business entities operating in the United States.

Employer Identification numbers can be obtained through third party resources such as Legal Zoom. These third-party providers request your EIN on your behalf but it takes several weeks to process. These providers also tack on an extra fee for processing your application to the IRS. If you are using a third-party resource to process your corporation or LLC documents they may also offer to process your EIN at the same time. Alternatively, you can request an EIN directly from the IRS website (www.irs.gov) or by phone, fax and postal mail. The online application validates your information during the session and your EIN is issued immediately.

Understand Insurance Requirements

Operating and owning any business, including a home inspection services, comes with many risks. While the formation of a corporation or a limited liability company can give you some protection you are never fully protected from your actions. Sometimes people are quick to react when they think they have been cheated or if something they own has been damaged. As a result, there are three types of insurance that home inspectors should obtain prior to opening the business: errors and omissions, general liability and automotive insurance.

Errors and omissions (E&O) is a professional liability insurance policy. This policy helps protect a professional service by providing individuals or companies from the full cost of defending a claims made by a client and damages awarded by a law suit. This coverage looks at the alleged failure to perform a particular service provided by the policyholder. Professional liability insurance is generally set up based on a claims-made basis which means that the policy only covers claims made during the policyholder's policy period. Claims that are related to incidents occurring before the coverage started may not be covered unless a retroactive date was included in the policy. This retroactive date is often the first day of coverage from the original E&O policy put in place when your business started.

General liability insurance helps protect the home inspector from being sued by third parties for negligence. When you are inspecting a home there is a risk of damaging the property and putting other people at risk of injury or loss. The general liability policy will pay compensation should you cause loss or damage during the home inspection process.

Automotive insurance is primary used to provide financial protection against physical damage and/or bodily injury resulting from a vehicle collision. It is important to have this coverage for your car or truck to help protect you from any liability traveling to and from the inspection. Additionally, something could happen with your vehicle when it is parked in the street or driveway of the property you are inspecting.

Workman's compensation insurance is another type of insurance that may not be required for companies with less than three employees. If you are a single inspector operation you may not need to obtain a workman's compensation policy. As you grow your business and add inspectors the cost of obtaining a workman's compensation policy should be taken into consideration.

Be sure to purchase as much E&O, general liability and automotive coverage as you can afford. Obtaining a one-million-dollar policy in each category is in your best interest as some of the properties that you are inspecting may cost at least that much. The following is a short list of some carriers that offer E&O and general liability coverage for home inspectors:

- Allen Insurance Group [www.allenins.com]
- Home Inspectors Insurance Solutions [www.inspectors.locktonaffinity.com]
- InspectorPro Insurance Program [www.inspectorproinsurance.com]
- Landy [www.landy.com]
- North American Professional Liability Insurance Agency (NAPLIA) [www.naplia.com]
- Organization of Real Estate Professionals (OREP) [www.orep.org]

Conform to State and Local Licensing

Most states require a person to obtain a home inspectors license prior to inspecting residential properties for a fee. The steps involved in obtaining a home inspector's license varies from state to state. If you happen to live in a state that does not require a license I recommend that you take a reputable home inspection course and pass the National Home Inspectors Exam [www.homeinspectorexam.org] prior to launching your home inspection service. This will give you credentials in states that do not require a home inspector's license.

Legislation enacted in the licensing states regulate the process of obtaining a home inspector's license. Most of these states have a list of approved home inspection courses to choose from. Once you have completed the course and passed their examination the next step is to pass the state appointed exam. Many states use the National Home Inspectors Exam and other states have their own exam. Sometimes there is an additional state requirement of performing or shadowing a certain number of home inspections prior to obtaining your license. Research what the home inspector licensing requirements are in your state and then call the regulating commission to verify what is required. The following is a recent list of state regulations.

- Alaska Licensure (Chapter 134 SLA enacted in 2003)
- Arizona Certification (Title 32, Chapter 1 enacted in 2002)
- Arkansas Registration (Act 1328 of 2003Current regulations as of 9/16/2005)
- California Trade practice act (Chapter 338) enacted in 1996
- Connecticut Licensure (Public Act No. 99-254 enacted in 2000)
- Florida Legislature (House Bill 713 during the 2010 Legislative Session)
- Georgia Trade practice act (Chapter 3, Title 8 enacted in 1994)
- Illinois Licensure (225 ILSC 441 enacted in 2001)
- Indiana Licensure (P.L. 145 enacted In 2004)
- Kansas (KS ST 58-4502)
- Kentucky Licensure (KRS 198B.700 enacted in 2004)
- Louisiana Licensure (Chapter 17-A of Title37 enacted in 1999)
- Maryland Licensure (Chapter 470 enacted in 2001)
- Massachusetts Licensure (Chapter 146 enacted in 1999)
- Mississippi Licensure (Chapter 71 enacted in 2001)
- Montana Trade Practice Act (Chapter 14, Title 30 enacted in 1999)
- Nevada Certification (NRS 645D.120 and NAC 645D.210 enacted in 1997)
- New Hampshire Licensure (Senate Bill 212)
- New Jersey Licensure (Chapter 8, Title 45 enacted in 1998)
- New York Licensure (Chapter 461 of the Laws of 2004)
- North Carolina Licensure (Chapter 143, Article 9F enacted in 1993)
- North Dakota Registration (HB 1507 enacted in 2005)

- Oklahoma Licensure (Section 858-622 of Title 59 enacted in 2001)
- Oregon Certification (ORS 701.350, 355 enacted in 1997)
- Pennsylvania Trade Practice Act (Act 114 of 2000, Title 68 enacted in 2000)
- Rhode Island Licensure (Chapter 65.1 enacted in 2000)
- South Carolina Licensure (Title 40, Chapter 59, Article 3 enacted in 1996)
- South Dakota Licensure (Chapter 36-21C enacted in 2000)
- Tennessee Licensure (2005 Public Act Chapter 65 enacted in 2006)
- Texas Licensure (Title 113A, Article 6573a, Section 23 enacted in 1991)
- Virginia Certification (Virginia Certified Home Inspectors Regulations enacted in 2001)
- Washington Licensure (SB 6606 enacted in 2008)
- West Virginia Certification (WV Code, Chapter 29, Article 3, Section 5b(c), Legislative Rule, Title 87, Series 5 enacted in 2006)
- Wisconsin Certification (Chapter 440.97 enacted in 1998)

In addition to having a state issued home inspector's license many municipalities also require companies to obtain a local business license. This business license is a permit issued by a local government agency that allows individuals or companies to conduct business within their geographical jurisdiction. The fees collected by the municipalities is essentially a tax to help cover the administration costs of running the local government.

Open Business Banking Accounts

In an effort to protect your personal assets you should set up business banking accounts for your home inspection business. These business accounts will be used for all income and expenses related to your home inspection business. It is very important not to mix your personal spending with your business expenses. If you do pay for personal expenses from your business accounts you are essentially "piercing the corporate vale" and opening yourself up personally for business related liabilities.

Open a business checking account in the name of your limited liability entity. This entity name will be on your account and at the top of your checks. Most banks will require that you already have your Employer Identification Number (EIN) in place before you open an account. The EIN is used in lieu of your Social Security Number (SNN) on the account. As discussed earlier an EIN can be obtained from the Internal Revenue Service (IRS). Your business checking account will be the primary vehicle for all incoming and outgoing cash used for your home inspection business.

It is also a great idea to open a business savings account with the same bank so that you can easily transfer money between your checking and savings accounts. Your home inspection business will have seasonal fluctuations of sales so having a business savings account can be very useful. From February to May there is traditionally a strong demand for home inspections. This is also another swell of demand between August and October. During these seasonal peaks you should be transferring extra cash to your business savings account to cover expense during the slower months.

Another helpful tool for your business is to have a business credit card. Banks usually issue a Visa or MasterCard for business accounts. The best use of a business credit card is to protect you from the liabilities of using your checking account debit card. A general rule is to never let your debit card leave your hand during a transaction. Examples of this would be at a restaurant where the waiter takes your card away from the table or using the card electronically over the internet. Credit cards have extra protection against fraud and the best part is that your checking account cannot be tapped in to directly from fraudulent activity.

Establish a Merchant Account

A Merchant Account is a type of bank account that allows a business to accept payments from clients using their debit or credit cards. It is important to make it convenient for your clients to pay you for your services. Many people like to use credit cards for high ticket items in order to rack up points for travel and other types of rewards. Since most home inspectors don't have a retail location, they need to have the ability to process credit card transactions either online or in person. One method is for the client to pre-authorize their card online during the home inspection scheduling process. The other option is to collect and process your client's credit card in person at the location of the home inspection.

When selecting a merchant service, you have a couple options. First you should check with the same bank that you opened your business accounts to see if they have in-house merchant services. Meet with their representative and review all of the fees involved in the service and how it can be integrated into your scheduling process and in to your business checking account. Other option is to look at third party providers of merchant services. A lot of research and questioning about fees should be part of your due diligence process for selecting the best merchant services provider for your home inspection business.

Choose a Communication Platform

One of the most important tools needed to operate your business is a computer. The best option in the last few years has been to use a laptop so that you can take it with you while you are away from the office. A Windows based PC with Microsoft Office has been the staple for most small business owners for many years. However, in the last few years business owners are considering new offerings of in-the-cloud services. Google Apps is a good example of this as they are offering word processing, spread sheets and other office related applications online so that they are assessable from many different devices and locations. Microsoft is now making a strong push for cloud-based office solutions with the release of Office 365.

The next most important thing related to your computer is the ability to connect to the internet. Home based businesses generally have two options for high-speed connections. One of the most common is connecting to the internet through your local cable TV company. With this option you get some of the highest speeds available in residential areas. The other option is to obtain internet service through your local telephone company. If the local telephone service has fiber optic cables in close proximity of your home, they can generally provide high speed connections similar to what you can get from a cable service provider. However, if the service is still coming through traditional phone wires the connections speeds are dramatically slower with DSL technology. If DSL is your only option it can still work for your home inspection business but it is not ideal. A new player in home-based internet services is the wireless phone companies such as Verizon Wireless and AT&T. The only drawback to these new services is that you pay for the amount of data passing through the system. Cable and DSL internet service providers offer unlimited data transfer.

Tablets have been around for a few years and have found a place in the business world. I purchased my first Android based tablet about two years ago but ended up giving it to my wife because I found it limiting to what I wanted to get done in the field. It was good to quickly check emails and use internet-based applications. What I found, however, is that the tablet could not do some of the things that a PC can do. Lately manufactures have come to the rescue and have devices that function both like a PC and a tablet.

Using a smart phone in your business is a must. To have the ability to answer the phone from wherever you are located, respond to emails and be able to text is very important. Your phone can also become your data hub (hot spot) for any wireless devices that you may be using while away from your office. One nice thing about having a wireless hub separate from your phone is that you can run several devices at once and not have your data interrupted while speaking on the phone. Another advantage of the separate hub is that it doesn't put an additional drain your phone's battery.

Choosing an email system is another important step before you launch your home inspection business. While many small businesses still use Microsoft Outlook, there are also in-the-cloud options as well. Google Apps allows you to use many different platforms to connect to your email and calendar. You can use your PC, smart phone and tablet to read and respond to your emails. Microsoft is attempting to keep up with these cloud-based services with Office 365 and new Windows based tablets and smart phones.

Backup Important Documents

Most home inspectors are single person operations and keep all of their important documents on their PC. A good practice is to create a folder on your PC for each home inspection you perform. Inside the folder are the photos from the inspection, a copy of your home inspection report and a signed copy of the inspection agreement.

Larger mult-inspector firms may have a server that all of the individual computers connect to. Important documents are backed up on their servers. If you are saving important documents to your PC's hard drive you should implement a routine backup procedure. One option is to have an external hard drive to copy your files to on a regular basis. Another option is an online backup service such as Carbonite [www.carbonite.com] to automatically store your data. These services automatically back up your files to their servers. If you lose a file or if your computer crashes you can retrieve your important documents from online backup service.

Finalize Your Inspection Agreement

The inspection agreement is a very important element of your home inspection process. It outlines the relationship between the home inspector and the client. One of the most important aspects of the agreement is that it defines the scope of work and the limitations of liability for the home inspector. Most home inspection associations have sample inspection agreements that you can use, copy and modify. Many home inspectors post a copy of their inspection agreement on their website. Once you have drafted your version of the inspection agreement you should have an attorney look it over to be sure that it complies with your state laws.

A copy of the inspection agreement my company used in South Carolina can be found in the Appendix. Upon review you will notice that our liability is limited to the fee paid for the inspection. Interestingly enough a recent South Carolina Supreme Court ruling upheld the legality of a limits of liability clause between a home inspector and their client. Business and contract laws vary per state so be sure that you and your attorney are comfortable with your agreement before using it in your state.

Choose Your Standards of Practice

Inspectors should have an inspection routine that is consistent on each home inspection they perform. The foundation for this routine should be wrapped around industry Standards of Practice (SOP). Each of the major home inspection organizations (ASHI, NAHI and interNACHI) have a published SOP for their members to follow. Copies of these standards are usually published on their respective websites.

- www.ashi.org/inspectors/standards/standards.asp
- www.nahi.org/about-us/nahi-standards-of-practice-code-of-ethics
- www.nachi.org/sop.htm

In many cases state governments also have their own home inspection standards. These states issued SOP's are often adopted from one of the major home inspection organizations and may have a few tweaks to them. In South Carolina, for example, the state standards are very close to the 2006 version of the ASHI SOP. In addition, South Carolina added about a half dozen extra items to the standards that cover window screens, screen doors, storm doors and kitchen appliances.

If your state has SOP's your inspection process should incorporate them. You are not limited, however, to the standards that you follow. Home inspectors are free to go beyond the standards of practice if they choose to do so. One example might include documenting the model and serial number of the heating, ventilation and air conditioning (HVAC) system and hot water tank to better determine the age of the equipment. Another example could be recording the temperature of the HVAC supply and return registers to document how the system is performing. I would encourage home inspectors to only add items to your inspection process that you believe adds value to your services. Anything beyond that is taking up your valuable time.

Establish Your Appointment Booking Strategy

There are many choices when it comes to scheduling your home inspection appointments and managing your appointment calendar. The traditional single inspector method is to hand out your business card with a cell phone number on it. Clients or real estate agents will call the inspector to schedule the appointment. As long as the inspector is not in a crawl space or not in front of a client, he or she should answer the phone. If it goes to voicemail, however, the odds are the person calling you will move on to the next home inspector on their list and book the appointment with that company.

When the inspector does answer the phone during a home inspection it can sometimes be difficult to book the appointment without having a computer or tablet in front of you. Answering the phone also disrupts the home inspection process and extends the time to complete the inspection at hand. If you are a single inspector operation and have a spouse that is involved in the business, they can answer the incoming phone calls and book the appointment while you are performing inspections. Larger home inspection companies often have an office location with a receptionist or scheduling person that can book the appointments. Another option for either single inspector or multi-inspector firms is to contract with a call center to book the appointments for you. The staff at these call centers are trained to professionally book your home inspection appointments and, in many cases, can up-sell some additional inspection services that your company may offer.

In today's world of smart phones, tablets and computers people expect to buy products or services at the moment that they are ready.

This is why having an online schedule system can be a very important strategy to secure home inspection appointments and reduce the amount of phone calls, return phone calls, mistakes taking notes and even worse double booking an inspection. An automated online scheduling tool can have several other advantages including managing multiple inspector's schedules, sending out automated emails, delivering the report and running business reports. Integrating the online scheduling feature into your website will make it easy for your clients and referring real estate agents to do business with you. Our company website [www.b-sureinspections.com] is a good example of how such an integrated online scheduling process works.

Choose Your Report Writing Platform

The home inspection report is the final product that you leave behind for your client. It is extremely important that this report reflects your professionalism and communicates your findings in the manner that you feel comfortable. The defects that you find during the home inspection process is the important information that your client and their real estate agent needs to create the home inspection repair addendum. This information should be easy to find in your report and is usually summarized somewhere at the beginning.

The layout of your home inspection report is also an important consideration. Your report should be easy to read and visually appealing. It should not include a bunch of technical jargon and "cover your butt" language. Another important aspect is to be sure that your report clearly follows the standards of practice that you choose to follow in your inspection process. When someone looks at your report there should be no doubt that you are indeed following industry standards. If your website and/or your visual inspection agreement states that you follow a certain standard you should be confident that your report represents this. Should a law suit be filed against you one of the most important things that an attorney will look at is what standards of practice that you claim to follow and does the report clearly reflect that you actually did follow these standards.

Home inspectors have many choices when it comes to report writing. They can create their own report using a word processor or purchase home inspection report writing software. For many years traditional home inspection software was purchased and then installed on your desktop or laptop computer. Some software developers are still selling this type of home inspection report writing software. Recently, cloud-based home inspection report writing software is gaining market share. When the report writing software is used in this environment it offers more options on when and how the reports can be created. Some software developers have versions of their software that work across many platforms such as personal computers, tablets or smart phones. Often a combination of these devices can be used to create the home inspection report. One of the most important things to consider when choosing your home inspection platform is whether or not you will have internet access in the field. If you inspect homes in remote locations you may have trouble connecting with cloud-based technology during your home inspection process.

Another big consideration is the cost of home inspection report writing software. Software that is purchased and installed on your computer will cost several hundred dollars and may be out of date in a few years. Cloud based report writing software is usually a subscription fee per inspection or based on a monthly rate. When I started my home inspection business, I used two different report writing products during the first couple years in business. The first one was installed on my computer and the second one was cloud based. While there were some unique advantages to both platforms, I ultimately decided to use a word processor for my report writing. This customizable word processing template was used at my company owned location and is now offered free of charge to our franchisees. With the word processing approach, we have the ability to control the content and layout in such a way that it is clear we are following the standards of practice outlined in my inspection agreement. A sample of our report can be found in the appendix. The following is a list of some of the most popular home inspection report writing software companies in no particular order.

- Palm-Tech [www.palm-tech.com]
- HomeGauge [www.homegauge.com]
- Home Inspector Pro [www.homeinspectorpro.com]
- ReportHost [www.reporthost.com]
- 3D Inspection System [www.3dinspection.com]
- ICHI [www.ichomeinspectionsoftware.com]
- HORIZON [www.discoverhorizon.com]

Obtain Your Inspection Tools

There really are not many inspection tools required to perform a professional home inspection. The following is a list of the essential home inspection tools that you should have:

- Folding ladder
- Flashlight(s)
- Electrical tester(s)
- IR thermometer
- Moisture meter(s)
- Elbow and knee pads
- Coveralls
- Respirator / face mask

As you grow your business you may want to acquire additional inspection tools to help you diagnose your visual observations. Some examples of these tools might include:

- Thermal imaging camera
- Borescope
- Video robot for crawl spaces
- Video drone for roofs

Choose Your Initial Inspection Services

The traditional home inspection for home buyers should always be your primary focus for your business. Nearly all people purchasing homes today are seeking to hire a home inspector. This is why home buyers are your primary target market. Pre-listing inspections are also becoming more popular as sellers are beginning to realize it is better to know what is wrong with their home and fix these issues before putting it on the market. Both of these inspection types should follow the same standards of practice that you have selected for your inspection business.

A new home inspector may be tempted to add other inspection services in an effort be all things to all people. These services can include, wind mitigation inspections, mold testing, radon testing, lead paint testing, pool and spa inspections, termite inspections, thermal imaging inspections, and more. I believe that some of these inspections may be very important depending on the regional location of your inspection business. However, before you add any of these additional inspection services be sure that you are properly trained and have the appropriate certifications. Additionally, for each extra inspection service that you add make sure that you include a separate inspection agreement because the scope of these services are not the same as the traditional home inspection.

Finalize Your Inspection Fees

Make sure that you price your home inspection services appropriately. Be sure to not price yourself too low or you will be working very hard and not earn what you deserve. Believe it or not most home buyers don't select a home inspector solely based on price. People actually express their values through how much they are willing to spend for a product or service. If they do not want to pay much for a home inspection it is an indication that they really do not value your service. Since your home inspection services is an offering of your skills, talents and personality you should expect to be well compensated. Make sure to set you fees at a rate that makes you feel valuable. When you do this you will not have any trouble converting conversations with potential clients into paying customers.

There is a place for offering special pricing packages or discounts to help motivate potential clients to buy your home inspection services. For example, offering a discount for using your online scheduling application could entice them to immediately act on your offer. There are also times when market conditions cause you to lower your prices because of economic conditions or intense competition from other inspectors. Don't offer too many discounts or special deals or your clients will feel that your standard pricing is not believable.

Make sure that you raise your inspection fees whenever you can. A good time to do this is when real estate activity starts to pick up early each calendar year. Another reason for raising your fees would be when you are in high demand or when you have improved your training or skills.

If someone bulks at your "high" price you might want to respond like this…

"We are neither the cheapest nor the most expensive home inspection service in town. Our schedule is nearly full each week because people appreciate what they receive from our services and don't mind paying for what they get."

When I started my business, my fees were based on what other inspectors in my market were charging. Many of my competitors published their inspections fees online and on their brochures. Initially my pricing was based on a base fee for the first 2,000 square feet and then an extra fee for each additional 500 square feet. Later our pricing is based on a flat fee for the first 1,000 square feet and then an extra $0.10 per square foot beyond that. We also charge and extra $50 for homes built on a crawl space. We encourage people to book their inspection appointment online to receive a $25 discount. The most important thing about setting your fees is to simply get started. My recommendation is to set your initial fees based on market rates and then increase your fees as your business grows.

Launch Your Business

Understand Why People Want to Hire You

As a home inspector you are in business to make money. In order to fill your calendar with home inspection appointments you must understand who your target market is. This is the person that hires and pays you for your inspection service so that you can pay your bills, buy food and save for retirement. Your target market is usually the person buying a home. Sometimes, however, it is actually the existing home owner that hires you to do a pre-listing inspection. Remember that the home buyer almost always chooses to include a home inspection as part of the offer to purchase a home. At this moment in time your target market (the home buyer), urgently needs your services. You now will have the opportunity to capture this client if you have implemented effective marketing strategies into your business plan.

Once you have been hired to inspect a home you must deliver exactly what your client needs. Whether or not they understand the home inspection process or not your service must deliver a thorough visual inspection of the property following acceptable standards of practice. Your job is to set proper expectations and fulfill your client's urgent need of knowing what the condition of the home is. After your service is complete you must deliver to your client a professional home inspection report in a timely manner. Your client's offer to purchase the property is contingent on many of the findings listed in your home inspection report. The real estate agent will sit down with them to review the report and decide what items should be included in the repair request addendum. A good home inspector never forgets why they are hired and who their target market is.

Many home inspectors come from a construction trade background and approach the business from a technical perspective. One of the most important things to remember is that a home inspector is neither a technician nor a building code official. Our role is to visually inspect the property for the person that hired you and present a list of defects per the standards of practice that they are following. That is all you were contracted to do. If the inspector truly understands this concept and is consistent, they will build a strong base of referrals from past clients and real estate professionals.

Build an Effective Website

Building a professional looking website with quality content will position you as the local home inspection expert. Before you get started you need to research the availability of website domain names. A best practice is to use your company name in your domain name that your website uses. For example, Ford Motor Company uses www.ford.com as their domain name. This domain name is simple and easy for customers to remember. So, if your company is John W. Smith Inspection Services you might want to secure the domain name www.johnwsmithinspectionservices.com if it is available.

When selecting a name for your company and securing the domain name you might ask what comes first. For me it was the availability of domain names that guided us into selecting B-Sure Inspections as our company name. My wife had the vision of the name B-Sure and the bee character. The "B" could represent Bingenheimer or it could simply be an abbreviation for "be at home with the right inspector." In order to finalize the company name it made sense to add a word or two that better describes the service being offered. Adding "inspection" or "home inspection" seemed logical. Since the domain www.B-Sureinspections.com was available I selected B-Sure Inspections for our company name. Later I further developed our logo with a house outline around the bee to better describe the service being offered. In addition, the tag line "America's Finest Home Inspection Service" better reinforced what my company offers.

A well-designed website can be a powerful tool for converting potential customers into paying customers. This website promotes your brand identity and should have a compelling offer to encourage people to hire you to inspect their home. Your website is a marketing platform that is available 24 hours a day and 7 days a week at precisely the time customers want to engage with you. The layout of your website should be easy to navigate and be focused on your target market: the home buyer or seller. The content of your web pages and your blog posts will determine whether your website will be effective or not. The layout should make it obvious where the visitor needs to go and what they need to do to book an inspection appointment.

Your online scheduling system should be integrated into your website to make it easy for your customers and referral sources to book inspection appointments. Remember the content of your website will help people move off the fence and hire you to inspect their home. However, the most important goal of your website is to make it easy for them to book inspection appointments. A well-designed website will drastically reduce the amount of phone calls that you receive because people can get the information they want and accomplish their urgent need, booking a home inspection appointment at their convenience.

To be sure visitors find your website make sure that it is listed with the major search engines. While Yahoo and Bing are important you should, however, focus your efforts on Google. Google dominate the search engine space with nearly 70% market share. Your website search engine optimization (SEO) should focus on ranking well on Google first. Optimize your website with key words that your customers and referral agents use to find home inspectors. Using an appropriate key word strategy to improve your website rankings is a constantly evolving process. Google occasionally changes their algorithm that determines how sites are found based on key words people use to find information.

Use as many strategies as possible to drive traffic to your website site. Your business card and all of your marketing materials should have your website domain address on them. Use the signature line in your email account to promote your website with a clickable link. When you publish articles online be sure to promote your website with clickable links. Participate in online groups or communities that are relevant to the home inspection industry. Find relevant marketing partners and exchange links to each other's websites. Take advantage of online press release sites when you have something new to announce about your business. Finally, consider pay-per-click advertising with Google AdWords to drive more traffic to your website.

Build Relationships of Trust

Successful home inspectors understand three important components of a business relationship. Both your clients and their referral sources need to know, like and trust you before they are willing to spend money for your services. All opportunities to sell your home inspection services start with a simple conversation. Your goal is to turn these conversations into relationships of trust with your potential clients. The secret with the sales process is that people prefer to buy from people they know, like and trust. The first part of this equation starts with knowing who you are and why you have decided to become a home inspector.

Spend some quiet time and ask yourself why you have decided to devote your valuable time and effort inspecting homes. Is it because you love everything about residential construction? Maybe it is that you get satisfaction from not only finding problems but also determining why a particular condition is causing the problem. Perhaps you enjoy helping people make informed decisions when purchasing real estate. You may find that you have a combination of reasons why you have decided to inspect homes for a living.

The next step is to become a likable home inspection expert in your market. Being likable starts with your professional appearance and your personality. You must be approachable and friendly without wasting anybody's time. There are several strategies to convey your expertise in the home inspection field. Sponsoring sales meetings in real estate offices is a good start. Teaching lunch-and-learn topics for real estate professionals, insurance agents and mortgage brokers takes it to the next level. If you have the credentials you can become a licensed instructor and teach continuing education classes for the real estate commission or department of insurance in your state. This puts you, the local home inspection expert, in front of dozens of referring professionals on a regular basis.

The trust component is perhaps the most important aspect of your know, like and trust formula. Trust is a feeling developed by your past and present actions. Your client must sense that you are the person that is looking out for them and not anybody else in the real estate transaction. It is also imperative that your referral source, usually the real estate agent, can trust that you are only looking out for their client as well. You must resist the temptation of conducting your inspection process to only benefit the real estate agent. If you feel that you are expected to look past things so that the agent can get a deal closed you should avoid working with this agent in the future. Do not ever compromise your integrity by looking out solely for the real estate agent's interests. Remember that building relationships of trust is a numbers game. There are ten times the amount of real estate agents out there that want you to look out for their buyer's interests first. Let your competitors inspect for the real estate agents that are looking out only for themselves.

Like it or not, the real estate agent is in the best position to introduce their clients to your services. Most standardized real estate contracts have a home inspection clause in the real estate purchase agreement. The home buyer is required to either waive their right to a home inspection or commit to hiring a home inspector usually within a limited time frame. In most cases the buyer will ask the real estate agent which home inspector to use as soon as the paperwork is signed.

I have found that most professional real estate agents will not "recommend" any one particular home inspector or home inspection company. In order to limit their liability, they may offer a short list of inspectors or hand their client some business cards / brochures from local inspection companies. This is the very reason why real estate professionals need to know that you exist. This is why these agents must already know, like and trust that you will look out for their clients. Several testimonials that demonstrate how we have built a know, like and trust relationship with our clients and referral sources can be found in the appendix.

Develop Your Personal Brand

The personal brand that you develop defines who you are and why you are a unique home inspector. It must clearly express why you have chosen to dedicate your life to serving home buyers and sellers. The brand that you develop allows you to distinguish yourself from the other home inspectors in your market. Developing your personal brand may seem a bit strange. The only brand I could claim when I started my home inspection business was that I was a licensed builder. During the first few months in business my reputation of conducting thorough home inspections and presenting the findings in a non-threatening way became my new personal brand.

The personal brand you develop helps make you known for your skills, talents and past experiences. This brand defines what you stand for and must let people see that you are authentic and memorable. In the process of developing your personal brand you need to create a statement about who you are and what you do for a living. This statement lets people know exactly who you are and what you can do to help them. Your personal statement should come from your heart so that it is authentic. Clients know when you are sincere and this is the very moment when they decide to spend money for your services. Be sure to reflect on what your personal brand is and develop a tag line that is unique for you.

It took me three years to develop my personal brand tagline. When I left the home building industry to start my home inspection business, I changed my title on LinkedIn from "Director of Purchasing" to "Entrepreneur." A few years later when I was approached to be a Google Helpouts expert they asked for a tagline for my listing. *The Home Inspection Guru* popped in to my mind as a fitting description of my home inspection talents and abilities.

Your personal brand must express that you are the premier home inspector in your market. You must look and act like a professional at all times. From what you wear to what your promotional materials say and look like is extremely important. You must have quality business cards, effective brochures, wear collared shirts with logos, have a professional looking website, use email addresses with your domain name and display your testimonials everywhere. These testimonials are the social proof that you are an endorsed professional home inspector.

Your business card design and use is essential. You risk being perceived as unprofessional if you don't have a card available when you are engaging with potential clients and referral sources. Exchanging business cards during home inspections and networking events is a common business ritual. Every time you meet someone new hand them your card. Also, during the home inspection be sure to hand your card to everyone present. Leave your card on the counter just like the real estate professionals do when they show a home. You never know, the seller may be looking for an inspector for their next home purchase!

My marketing materials have changed dramatically over the years. My first generation of business cards and brochures didn't even have a logo. My first business card just had an image of the bee with the magnifying glass along with my company name and contact information. My first tri-fold brochure simply had the company name at the top of the cover and a large bee on the cover. The remaining content was a bunch of worthless information that nobody was going to take to the time to read anyway. After listening to friends, clients and referral sources I developed a rack card that is straight to the point. I now have a company logo and a list of reasons to choose our company to inspect their home. The discount for scheduling online that is displayed on all of my marketing materials is the offer that encourages people to take action now.

Talk about What You Do

It is important to be comfortable talking with people about what you do for a living. You should always strive to create a meaningful dialogue during your conversations with potential clients and referral sources. The personal statement that you develop for why you are a home inspector can help you develop comfortable conversations. You need to actively engage in a conversation that elicit questions from the other person rather than having them listen to your "thirty second" elevator speech.

When you are having conversations with people be sure to identify the most critical problems that your audience is facing. Develop a list in your mind of how you can solve these problems and create opportunities for them to conduct business with you. You must demonstrate the most relevant reasons on how you can solve their urgent needs.

Many home inspectors do not see themselves as salespeople. Sometimes this is because they view the sales process as unethical and manipulative. If this is the way you feel than you need to move past this perspective and convince yourself that you are worthy of the money that clients pay you for your services. The sales process is about building relationships of trust with your potential clients. It is about having a sincere conversation that allows you to let these potential clients know what you can do to help them. You are simply making them aware of your services which they already need, want and desire. Think in terms of providing solutions to their problems. When you approach it this way they will beg you to work for them. Through these conversations you can become a lifelong consultant for their real estate needs.

Grow Your Business

TM

Join Networking Groups

The purpose of networking is to connect your business offering with other people. When you are participating in networking groups or meetings you should focus on sincerity and freely giving and sharing your knowledge and expertise. When you network you are building and deepening mutually beneficial relationships with potential clients and referral sources. Done properly you are making lasting connections that will drive more business to your doorstep.

When you are attending networking, events ask yourself how you can start and continue friendly conversations with people that you have never met before. Work to put other people at ease and listen attentively so that you can recognize their needs. Make sure you provide value and offer advice to help them be more successful. Be sincere and express generosity during your conversations. Make genuine connections that lead to strong future business opportunities.

Your reoccurring primary networking efforts should target strong referral sources such as real estate agents, insurance agents and mortgage brokers. These business professionals can generate a lot of leads for your home inspection business so it is imperative that they get to know, like and trust you. Networking with other business professionals such as termite inspectors, mold and remediation contractors, electricians, plumbers, heating and cooling contractors is also very important. When you are engaged with other business professionals it gives you an opportunity to connect and share resources. This shared knowledge and information can help you and your new connections grow businesses together.

The possibilities for meeting new people are endless. Any time you're sharing your connections, knowledge, and compassion with people you're networking. Any time that you are learning more about what others do, you're networking. Anytime you link or connect two people together you're networking. Informal networking opportunities can be a casual chat in line at the store or speaking in the yard with your neighbor. Formal networking opportunities can be at Toastmasters International events, Chamber of Commerce meetings, networking or leads groups and trade associations.

To be honest my home inspection business was up and running nearly two years before I joined my first networking group. This group was informal and did not have a charter or a strong set of rules to follow. There were about twenty members in this leads group and we met at a local real estate office every other week. I really enjoyed the relationships built during the two years that I was part of that group. I did receive some referrals from the group but the biggest thing that I gained was getting to know other business owners and sharing ideas on marketing and obtaining more clients.

During my third year in business, I joined a Business Networking International (BNI) group. This organization is the world's largest referral network organization. Weekly attendance is mandatory and lots of documented referrals are expected. While I found this organization very time consuming it was still worthwhile to make some important business connections and generate some new home inspection clients.

Develop a Direct Outreach Program

The purpose of a direct outreach program is to let people know that you exist. The first step is to make contact and develop a relationship with as many people as you can. Once you have met a person at a networking event or have done business with them in the past you now have permission to market to them. Without first developing this relationship you are wasting your valuable time and resources marketing to someone that does not know who you are.

There is no doubt that the real estate professionals has tremendous influence over their clients. Their client is the person that is seeking to hire a home inspector. Keep in mind that the goals and motivation of the real estate agent are not the same as the person buyer or selling the home. The home buyer is looking to make an informed decision on a big financial investment while the home seller is looking for a punch list of issues they need to deal with before putting their home on the market. The real estate agent, however, is a business person that wants a deal to go through so that they can get paid their commission. Real estate agents have a fiduciary responsibility to look out for their client but remember that they don't get compensated for their efforts until a property has closed.

In order to avoid any question of your objectivity in the home inspection process you need to only focus on the condition of the home. The home inspector's goal is to represent the condition of the home as accurately as possible to the home buyer or the seller if it is a pre-listing inspection. Avoid any temptation to make the home sound better than it is just to make the real estate professional happy. On the other hand you don't want to scare you client with your legitimate findings. Even if there are a lot of things wrong with the home you can still present the facts in a non-threatening way. Be objective and professional and you will develop respect with each of your clients and their respective real estate agents.

To be efficient with a direct outreach program the home inspector also needs to look at the financial implications of targeting your audience. It is more cost effective to target and market to that real estate agent verses the actual home buyer or seller. If you did find a way to connect directly with a home buyer or seller and performed their inspection you might also obtain one other referral to a friend over the next year or so. So if your average inspection fee is $300 you could earn $600 in a years' time from the effort you made marketing to that one new client. However, if you are networking with a top producing real estate agent you might receive ten home inspection referrals during that same amount of time. With those ten inspections you could earn $3,000 in inspection revenue verses the $600 for the same amount of marketing effort.

In order to be successful with your direct outreach strategy you need to first learn as much as possible about the people that you want to build relationships with. Seek to find common interests that you might have with these people. Learn what motivates them. Research and find out what they have accomplished in their professional career. Find out who their competition is and whom their peers are. Create unique benefits that you can offer in this new relationship. Finally ask yourself what your current status or role is in this person's professional life. Social media may be your best resource for obtaining information about the very people that you want to build business relationships with. You can use LinkedIn, Facebook and Google+ to make connections and find those common interests that you have.

Make a short list of people that you would like to develop professional relationships with. These are the people that can quickly connect you with your next potential client: the home buyer or home seller. The most obvious to make are top selling real estate agents. However, you might also consider mortgage brokers and insurance agents because they engage with home buyers and sellers on a regular basis. This list of influencers that you develop will have a significant impact on your business through direct referrals.

Once you have your list in place systematically contact one person each day. Use the phone, social media, email, postal mail or some other means to make the connection. Move that person to the bottom of your list and make connection with the second person the next day. Keep moving through your list until you get to the bottom and go through it again. Use a different method to connect on your second and third attempt. Find a way to grab the attention of your new audience. A unique or wacky approach will help you stand out in the crowd. With a dedicated effort your actions are the key to a successful direct outreach program that will help fill your calendar with home inspection appointments.

Create Strong Referral Sources

If you work to develop deeper relationships with every real estate agent and client that you meet, they will tell their friends about you. When this begins to happen your client, base potential multiplies automatically. This is the simplest and most inexpensive marketing strategy for your home inspection business. An organized referral program can triple or quadruple the number of referrals coming your way each year. This strategy will connect you with the very people that will one day need your services. Referral generated clients are more loyal and willing to pay more for your services than other people.

In order to fill your calendar with inspection appointments you need to seek out new referral sources each and every week. Identify the top potential referral sources in your market. Find out where you can meet and network with these people. Make sure all of your referral sources know how to book inspection appointments with you. Be sure that it is easy to book appointments with your company.

Make sure that you practice and polish your communication skills. Speak to your referral sources with lots of expression and show them that you are passionate about what you do for a living. Smile and make eye contact during your conversations. Always be confident during these conversations and when they start to speak, be quite and listen to their needs. Once you begin speaking with your referral sources on a deep and personal level, they will see you as a real person and not just the inspector. They will develop a higher level of respect for you and see the true person that you are.

Once your business growth is underway look for patterns in the referrals that you are receiving. Who sent you most referrals? How did they find and contact you? Are you keeping in touch with your referral sources on a regular basis? Keeping in touch with your referral sources is much easier than developing brand new relationships. Real life testimonials from our clients and referral sources can be found in the appendix.

Select Your Keep-in-Touch Strategy

Putting together and implementing a keep-in-touch strategy is perhaps the most important marketing activity you will do. There is plenty of research that proves that you need to connect with potential referral sources or clients several times before they are comfortable hiring you. Without a system to automatically keep-in-touch with your potential clients or referrals sources you will miss out on earning money from the very people that need your inspection services.

Once you have developed a relationship with or have done business with a client or referral source you now have permission to communicate or follow-up with them. Because of your relationship your clients and referral sources will pay more attention to the marketing message that you are sending them. Keep in mind that some people don't like to be spammed with online marketing materials. Even if they do have a relationship with you they may be overwhelmed with emails so they should always give them a way to opt out of your communications.

You must ensure that the content you share with your potential clients is relevant, interesting, current and valuable. Any real estate industry information that you choose to share must be relevant and not widely known. Strategies, tips and other marketing techniques are good things to send to the real estate agents that are producing referrals for you.

Much of your keep-in-touch strategy should be based on giving away free content. The balance is made up of offers to schedule home inspections with your company. Be sure to send out information that is fun, unique and unusual so that you stand out. If you send out special announcements about your home inspection business make sure it is relevant and presented as a learning tool.

Once you have great content to share with your referral sources and/or clients you must choose the best way to deliver it. Electronic newsletters are the easiest and most cost-effective way to keep in touch with a large number of people. Be careful, however, with the frequency that you send electronic communications. If you send out content too often you might end up in a spam folder and not have a chance to get your message delivered. Used wisely you can sell your services while at the same time deliver great content that they are interested in. When done properly you will position yourself as the home inspection expert in your market.

Speak in Front of Referral Sources

Your speaking strategy is used to get you in front of your clients and referral sources and position yourself as a home inspection expert. When you deliver presentations you express your knowledge, talents and strengths as a home inspector. When you share your knowledge and expertise it becomes a rewarding experience for you and your audience. The people that you share information with will leave your presentation knowing something new.

Speaking in front of real estate agents is perhaps the most effective use of your presentation efforts. Your local Realtors Association is a good place to start. See if there is a way for you to get involved. Most associations require their members to earn continuing education credits every year before the can renew their membership. Check out what topics are currently offered and determine what it takes to get qualified to teach these continuing education classes.

Another way to get in front of real estate agents it to sponsor a sales meeting in a local real estate office. Sponsoring these meetings is one of the easiest ways to get in front of a group of potential referral sources. Strategically pick a few offices to target for a speaking engagement. Ask the receptionist or office manager when the next sales meeting is and seek to obtain a commitment. Most real estate offices will give you 5 or 10 minutes to speak in exchange for sponsoring their meeting. Deliver a brief introduction and teach them something new. Keep it interesting and fun. Don't forget to bring some food because real estate agents love to eat!

Teaching lunch-and-learn classes is another great way to develop relationships with great referral sources. Similar to sponsoring sales meetings you need to book an appointment with the receptionist or office manager. On your scheduled day bring in some food and deliver your presentation. The topic does not need to be exclusive to home inspections. You can share anything with the agents that would help them grow their businesses. These presentations are key to giving new referral sources a reason to know, like and trust you. They will now remember you when they need your services.

Write about What You Do

Writing about what you do can help develop your reputation as a home inspection expert. You want people to think about you first when they need a home inspector. Writing short articles online can give you visibility and drive more traffic to your website to book inspection appointments. The more people that find and read your articles the better chance you have of converting them to paying customers.

When you start to draft an article, you need to choose an ideal topic and create a title that grabs the attention of your audience. Sometimes you may not even come up with the best title until you have finished writing your article. As soon as you have an idea for an article you just need to sit down and start writing. Do not worry about getting it perfect the first time. The most important thing is to just start typing. You will likely make changes to the article a few times until you feel like it is well written.

Each day that you are out inspecting a home there is at least a dozen things that you observed that could be content for a great article. Loose electrical outlets, rusty condensate drain pans, flues with negative slope, leaks around toilets, foggy windows, etc. Jot down a word or two when inspecting to remind you of the topic that you could write about later. After you finish your home inspection report type up a quick draft for your article. Edit and improve the content the following day. Finalize you article the third day. Be sure to publish your article the next day.

Developing an attention-grabbing title for your article is very important. The title determines whether your article will be read or not. People do not bother reading articles if the title does not intrigue them to do so.

Start your article with a brief introduction that contains the purpose of your story. It should summarize what is coming up in the body of your article. This introduction should tie in and build on the topic that you presented in the title. This introduction must explain why your article is important to the reader. If you address what is in it for the reader in the introduction you will keep their attention and they will continue reading.

In the body of your article, you must fulfill the promise that was made in the title and introduction of your story. Stay with one idea in each paragraph that you write. Limit each paragraph to two or three sentences. Using subheadings when appropriate can keep the reader engaged. Adding lists to your content is also effective in grabbing the attention of the reader and keeping them interested. Optimize the likelihood of people finding your article online by using key words throughout your story. Sum up what you wrote with a conclusion at the end of your article. Make sure it is easy for the reader to remember your main theme to reinforce the content in your reader's mind.

Once you have mastered the article writing process you are ready to publish your work. Blogging is an excellent way to quickly get your articles out in front of the public. You can publish you articles on your own website blog or on public blogging platforms. When you write on your own website you are reinforcing your expertise to people that are visiting your website. You want to convert visitors to paying customers by publishing quality relevant content in your blogs. Blogging on public sites has its own unique advantage. If the blogging site that you publish your articles is popular you can add backlinks in your article that will drive more traffic to your website and help boost your search engine rankings.

Once you have mastered sharing your written work online you should consider writing articles for print publications. Most newspapers are looking for good content from experts in their respective fields. Doctors, home improvement and landscape contractors often have articles in your local paper. So, why not a qualified home inspector? Editors need articles to fill their pages with good content that is informative and entertaining for their readers.

Finally, a press release can also help get the word out about your services. If you launch a new inspection service or receive a new certification a press release can drive a lot of traffic to your website. Your goal with the press release is to increase the number of visitors on your website and convert them to paying customers with compelling offers and quality website or blogging content.

Implement a Social Media Strategy

Social media is a relatively new environment for people to engage with one another. The big players in recent years have been Facebook, Twitter, YouTube and LinkedIn. Google+ is a relatively new player in social media and will likely have a huge impact on business to consumer marketing. When you engage in online social networking you must be willing to commit time to it and be consistent. Never outsource your company's social media marketing. You need to personally show up and do it yourself. Remember, it is called social media for a reason: it's social. Make time to post new comments, monitor other people's comments and participate in their conversations.

When you engage online in social media you are networking. Your efforts must be both quantitative and qualitative. You can enhance your brand identity through positive, professional and valuable interactions online. When you use social media consistently and appropriately you will see new customers or referral sources engage with your business when the need home inspection services.

Your ultimate goal is to find new clients and quality referral partners. You can use social media to earn credibility and visibility, announce events, promote your services, drive traffic to your website or bog, build email lists and develop relationships to create a base of raving fans of your home inspection business.

Facebook

There are two main components of Facebook: your profile and your page. In order to engage with people through Facebook you must first set up your personal profile. Once your profile is in place you can invite friends and begin to post your thoughts, photos and videos online. Your friends see your posts and you can view their posts. Commenting on posts, photos and videos on your news feed is where the social part of Facebook lives.

As a business owner you should consider creating your professional presence on Facebook in what is called a page. On this business page you can build your brand identity and professional image. People that find your page can "Like" it and become listed as a fan of your home inspection business. These fans will be able to see posts, photos and comments that you populate in their news feed. You need to effectively use both your profile and your business page in conjunction with each other in order to maximize your online networking efforts.

Use Facebook to showcase your home inspection expertise. Actively engage with potential customers and referral sources on a regular basis. Share your knowledge and compassion through this popular social media platform. Write about what you do with short posts and include a photo or video to grab attention. Make sure that you post useful information and ask provocative questions to compel your readers to respond. Always include links to your website in all of your posts.

Twitter

Twitter is basically a micro blogging site that allows you to communicate quickly with people that are following you. You can also select people that you are interested in following and keep up with their tweets in real time. Twitter users post updates, called tweets, in 140 characters or less. A big part of your Twitter strategy is to develop a following of targeted people who are interested in the content that you tweet. This is the same strategy you would use with a newsletter but the content is concise and timely. This social media platform allows you to stay in front of your target audience on a regular basis.

LinkedIn

LinkedIn is the professional or business alternative to Facebook. You can post your entire professional profile online and connect with people that you have done business with in the past. There is also an internal email application that allows you to communicate with your connections. You also have the ability to post your status in a similar fashion to Facebook.

Through LinkedIn you can make professional connections and position yourself as the home inspection expert in your market. LinkedIn also has groups where people join and create discussions about topics they are interested in. People can add their contributions to discussions that they are interested in to share real life experiences with others.

YouTube

The emergence of YouTube has made it possible for small businesses to reach potential customers quickly and affordably. As a result, the use of online videos to market and promote a business or service has exploded over the past few years.

When developing content for your home inspection videos begin with the end in mind. Consider what your potential customers want or need. The content is the most important element of your video strategy. Developing quality content is critical so that you are adding value and positioning yourself as an expert in the home inspection industry.

Part of the magic of video marketing is the ability to expand your visibility and exposure through social media. Video is viral by nature and sharing your video across as many social media platforms as possible can extend the reach of your brand across the internet.

Make Money
Inspecting Homes

Establish a Weekly Routine

It is important to set a schedule for both your marketing and inspection activities. During the first year in business, you will be spending more time marketing your business than you will inspecting homes. As you enter your second and third year in business you will be inspecting a lot more than marketing. No matter how busy you get inspecting homes you still need to block out some time to market your services and get your office related activities done.

For marketing activities, you should block out two half days per week. I usually blocked out Tuesday mornings to visit targeted real estate offices. On Thursday afternoon I blocked out some time to right blogs and develop my newsletters. For the rest of the week, I was available to inspect homes in the mornings at 9:00 AM and afternoons at 2:00 PM. This gives me eight time slots to inspect homes during the week. I was also available on Saturday mornings on most weekends.

Whatever schedule you set on your calendar be sure that you stick to your plan. It is real tempting to give up your marketing activities in lieu of the opportunity to inspect homes during the busy seasons. I challenge you to stick with your marketing activities on a consistent weekly basis. If you get out of sync with your marketing you will find that demand for your services will drop during the slow seasons. With consistent marketing, however, you will have a better chance to keep your calendar filled with inspections all year long.

Writing an Effective Blog

Writing about what you do on a consistent basis will create more opportunities for people to discover your home inspection services. The term blog is short for the word web log. Blogs are a quick and easy way to write short stories about something you are interested in. The purpose of writing blogs online is to attract people to your business or service. The first step in writing an effective blog is determining a topic that someone would be interested in reading. Each day a home inspector encounters many defects during the inspection process. Each of these defects are documented in a photo that is included in the home inspection report. At least one of these photos could be a great story or educational opportunity to blog about. The cool thing about having photos from your inspections is that you can include them in your blog. Pictures capture people's interest which can lead them to take the time to read your story.

Once you have decided what your blog topic is going to be take a few minutes and determine what key words would help your story be found on the internet. Keywords are a grouping of a few words that someone is likely to use when searching for content online. For example, if you want to learn more about why your tub spout is dripping you might use the following keywords:

- "tub spout leak"
- "dripping tub spout"
- "leak at tub spout"

When you type in these words in the search box of your browser several links for YouTube videos, websites and blogs will appear in the search results. The more unique your topic and keywords are the more likely your blog will appear near the top of the search results.

The next step is to write the body of content for your blog. Typically, a blog can simply be three paragraphs. The first paragraphs tell the story about what you found on an inspection. The second paragraph tells the reader why it is important. The final paragraph will give the reader suggestions on how to fix or avoid the problem in the first place. It really does not need to be any more complicated than that. Each paragraph usually contains four to five sentences.

Search engines prefer blogs that have at least 300 words and at least one embedded photo. Your keywords should also be embedded in the title of your blog and at least three times inside the content of the blog. If you incorporate these strategies your blog will have a better chance of being discovered on the internet. There are several blogging platforms available and many of them are free. Look for blogging platforms that have a big following and a lot of traffic. Activerain.com for example is a popular real estate blogging platform. There are numerous blogging platforms online that you should consider using to drive traffic to your website. Many home inspectors also have websites built on a blogging platform. If you create good unique blogging content on topics relative to home buyers or home sellers you have a much better chance of converting online readers in to paying customers.

Booking Appointments

All of your marketing efforts should drive people to book home inspections with your company. Your business cards, rack cards, flyers, newsletters, blogs, educational events and sponsorships should engage people with an offer to do business with you. For many years the traditional way of booking appointments was for a real estate agent or home buyer to call you on the phone. The traditional questions people ask when they call are:

1. "What is your inspection fee?"
2. "When are you available?"

When you answer the phone, you should be prepared to answer these questions and then give them a few more reasons to hire you. The odds of these callers booking with you is about 50% at this point because they will tell you they are calling several inspectors. If you do not answer your phone the odds of them booking with you is nearly zero percent. Some will leave you a voicemail but by the time you call them back they have likely already booked with someone else.

Closing the deal on the phone is not an easy task. I found that most people calling on the phone are simply looking for the cheapest price. In the early days of running my inspection business I let people talk me into lowering my fees. In the early weeks it made sense because I wanted to work and earn some money. Then one day I found myself in a tight crawl space thinking how crazy I was to let this customer talk me in to inspecting this home for $235. A professional home inspector has legitimate expenses and taxes to pay just like any other business owner. It didn't take me long to realize that working for cheap would barely pay the bills and not leave much money in my pocket.

To close a deal on the phone you need to be professional and give your potential customer a reason to do business with you. You should have a unique selling position that sets you apart from your competition. You may offer discounts for booking the inspection from your website. Offering military discounts for our heroes and their families may also be an additional incentive that will help capture some inspections. If you cannot answer your phone all of the time you should consider hiring a call center. A professional call center can answer all of your incoming calls especially when you are not available during inspections. These call centers are also trained to capture the sale and book the inspection on your behalf.

Today there is an alternative to booking inspection over the phone. Many inspection companies offer the ability to book inspections from their website or Facebook page. This technology allows real estate professionals or your potential home buyers the opportunity to check out your business and then book the inspection appointment when they are ready. One huge benefit of online scheduling is that people are no longer looking for a phone number, leaving messages and playing phone tag trying to book their inspection.

The online scheduling system allows people to see what your availability and fees are during the booking process. They enter some property information, some contact information and then choose the day and time for the inspection that works best for them. A good, simple and easy online scheduling system will dramatically reduce the number of incoming and outgoing phone calls. Less phone calls frees you up to concentrate on your home inspections and focus on marketing your business.

Develop Your Home Inspection Field Process

As a home inspection professional, you should deliver a consistent home inspection service at every inspection you perform. The following is an outline of the process we use in our Charleston, South Carolina market. Inspectors in other locations will certainly encounter some different foundation types and heating systems than we generally see in the South. You need to develop an inspection workflow that works best for your business and refine it as you experience real life situations in the field.

Prior to Leaving Your Home Office:
- Print your inspection order
- Print your field note sheets
- Print the invoice if the client has not already pre-authorized their credit card
- Print the inspection agreement if they have not approved it online

Arriving at Your Inspection Appointment:
- Be sure to arrive 10 to 15 minutes early
- Have your business cards and gift ready for your client
- Place the invoice and/or inspection agreement on a separate clip board for your client (if applicable)

- Put your digital camera in one pocket and your electrical tester in another pocket.
- While you are waiting on your client or the agent to arrive stand in the street, take a photo of the home and jot down some descriptions in your field notes

Greeting Clients and Agents:

- When the client and/or their agent arrives wait until they get out of their car, approach and introduce yourself with a warm smile and firm handshake
- Generate some small talk to break the ice: weather, traffic, location of the neighborhood, etc.
- As the agent and/or their client enters the home tell them that you will start your inspection process outside
- Remember that is not the inspector's responsibility to turn on the water, electrical or gas

Exterior Inspection Workflow:

- Walk up and down the street in front of the home until you have examined all of the visible roof
- Look around at neighboring homes at the condition of their roofs
- Walk up to the front right corner of the home and examine the exterior from the top to bottom
- Walk clockwise around the home examining the exterior finishes
- During your walk around the home visually inspect the hose bibs, electrical outlets, electrical service, gas meters and HVAC equipment
- Examine the rear roof that is visible from the ground
- When you arrive to the front right corner of the home walk around one more time to see if there is something you missed the first time

When You Enter the Home:

- Check to be sure the power, water and gas (if applicable) is on

- Check to be sure the water heater is on
- Check the drain line for the dishwasher and then turn it to the rinse cycle
- Prior to entering the attic examine all of the ceiling directly below the attic space

Attic Inspection Process:

- Inspect the pull-down stairs if applicable
- Carefully inspect every accessible part of the attic space
- Visually inspect the structure, roof sheathing, insulation, ventilation
- Visually inspect any plumbing supply and vent pipes, electrical wiring, water heating equipment and HVAC equipment or ducts

Interior Inspection Process:

- Pick a room on the top floor of the home and begin your room-to-room inspection routine
- Open/close all doors and windows
- Turn on/off all light switches
- Examine the ceilings, walls and trim
- Test the electrical outlets
- Move to the next room in a clockwise manner until you have checked everything on this level
- Move to the lower level of the home (if applicable) and repeat this process

Bathroom Inspections:

- Open/close all doors and windows
- Turn on/off all light switches
- Examine the ceilings, walls and trim
- Test the electrical outlets
- Turn the hot and cold water on/off at the sink
- Look for leaks under the sink
- Flush the toilet and lift the tank lid while refilling

- Look for leaks around the base of the toilet and at the tank
- Turn the tub/shower hot and cold water on
- Examine the tub/shower
- If there is a jetted garden tub fill it with water and turn it on

Kitchen Inspections:

- Open/close all doors and windows
- Turn on/off all light switches
- Examine the ceilings, walls and trim
- Test the electrical outlets
- Turn the hot and cold water on/off at the sink
- Look for leaks under the sink
- Open/close all cabinet doors and drawers
- Turn the oven on for a few minutes and then back off
- Turn the cooktop on/off
- Turn the microwave on/off
- Turn the exhaust fan on/off

Garage Inspections:

- Open/close all doors and windows
- Turn on/off all light switches
- Examine the ceilings, walls and trim
- Test the electrical outlets
- Visually inspect any hot water systems, electrical systems or HVAC systems
- Open/close the garage door

Crawl Space Inspection:

- Proceed slowly into the crawl space and become accustomed to your surrounds
- Travel to all accessible parts of the crawl space
- Examine all visible structural members
- Observe the insulation, moisture barrier and ventilation
- Note any moisture issues and determine why it is happening

- Visually inspect any plumbing supply and vent pipes, electrical wiring, water heating equipment and HVAC equipment or ducts

Basement Inspections:
- Visually inspect the structure, floor sheathing and insulation if visible
- Visually inspect any plumbing supply and vent pipes, electrical wiring, water heating equipment and HVAC equipment or ducts
- Open/close all doors and windows
- Turn on/off all light switches
- Examine the ceilings, walls and trim
- Test the electrical outlets

Presenting Your Findings to Your Client

When you are done with your inspection process it is time to present your finding to your client. Often the real estate agent is also there to listen and then set expectations on what the next steps are with their client. The way that you present your findings is critical to the success and reputation of the home inspector. There is absolutely no reason to be an alarmist and act like the authority figure in the room. The process of presenting your findings to the home buyer should be very simple. Present them with the facts and then get out of the way.

During my inspection process I take photos with an inexpensive digital camera. I use the display on the camera to walk the client through each discovery found during the inspection. Before I begin, I set the expectation that many of the photos that I take are just for documentation. The photos that show the issues discovered during the home inspection process will be included in the home inspection report. One by one I scroll through the photos and explain what my discoveries were. The key here is to only give an explanation of what they are looking at in the photo. If it is something they don't understand you give them a quick description in layman's terms.

When you are done showing them the photos begin your exit strategy. You want to get out of the way and let the real estate agent take it from here. Tell the client that you will email the report to them and you are available to answer any questions they may have once they have reviewed the report. One nice way to wrap things up with your client and get their minds off of your findings is to present them with a gift and thank them for their business. This gift does not need to be expensive and should always display your logo. Coffee cups, tumblers, stress balls and pens are always well received.

Taking Payments

Most of the time our clients pre-authorize their credit/debit card online prior to the inspection day. Their card will automatically be charged after the inspection has started. There is a cost to accept credit/debit card payments from your clients. The typical merchant fee for these transactions is approximately 3% of the sale or inspection fee. This can be a significant expense if your company is inspecting several hundred homes per year. However, customers like to earn travel or bonus rewards by using their cards and like the convenience as well. Inspectors that choose not to accept credit/debit cards will be missing out on significant inspection revenue.

When the client does not pre-authorize their credit/debit card online the inspector needs to be able to process payment in person at the inspection. The inspector should have the ability to process credit/debit cards on site. This can be done with a smart phone app or using your laptop computer. For the client that has concerns about processing a credit/debit card online you give them the option of paying cash or giving you a check. You can avoid the merchant fees when you accept cash or checks but you also need to factor in the time it takes to go to the bank and the possibility of a check bouncing every once and a while.

Sometimes a client or even their agent will ask if you are willing to get paid at closing. When this request is made it is usually because the seller has allocated some funds to the buyer for closing related costs. It is a business decision on whether you want to wait several weeks until closing to get paid. Another consideration is that the home may not close or the closing attorney may not include payment to the inspector on the closing statement. Our response to a request to get paid at closing has been to ask the client to charge the inspection fee to their credit card. Once we receive a check from the closing attorney, we write a check to our client to reimburse them for the inspection fee that was applied to their credit card.

Obtaining a Signed Inspection Agreement

The visual inspection agreement needs to be read and signed by each and every client. The best procedure is to send it to your client at the time the appointment was scheduled. Our online scheduling system automatically sends the inspection agreement to our client the day the inspection was booked online. This procedure gives our client time to read the agreement in advance. You should also give your client an opportunity to approve the agreement in advance as well. Capturing an electronic signature and approval online happens with more than 90% of our clients.

If the client does not approve the inspection agreement online the inspector needs to bring a printed copy to the inspection. After introducing yourself at the beginning of the inspection give your client a copy of the inspection agreement and ask them to read and sign it while you are performing the inspection. Tell them that it is the same document that was emailed to them and a copy of the agreement will also be included with their inspection report.

Report Writing Strategies

The home inspection report is the final product that your client receives from you. The report should be easy to read and clearly present your findings. It is also a great marketing product for your company because the client is likely to forward this to their agent and perhaps some of their friends. The client's agent is likely to forward your report to the seller's agent. If the seller's agent likes your report format, they may consider referring you to their future clients.

Your report format must look professional. In the report you must call out all significant deficiencies discovered during your inspection process. It is important that your report appears to clearly follow the standards of practice that your inspection agreement states that you follow. If the report does not clearly follow the standards of practice you risk exposure to litigation if something you missed is discovered later.

The basics of report writing include describing the components you inspected, identify problems, explain why it is important and advise on what to do about it. When you identify the problem, you tell your client what you saw and where is was located. The issue can be that the item is not functioning properly, is significantly deficient or it is unsafe. You should explain to your client why they should care and what implications may exist if it is not self-evident. It is also important to advise your client on what action to take if they do not know what to do. Typical actions are to request repairs, monitor the situation or request further evaluation by a trade specialty (electrician, plumber, heating and air contractor). Often it is the real estate agent that suggests to their client what actions to take which becomes the basis for the repair addendum.

Report Writing Procedures

Taking notes during the inspection is very important. Using a customized form on a clipboard during the inspection helps to be sure that you do not forget a component that you are required to inspect. Completing this form in its entirety can ensure that you are indeed following your chosen standards of practice. Taking digital photos during your inspection is also very important. I take photos of the major components (HVAC, hot water systems, electrical systems, etc.) to refer to during the report writing process. Taking photos of all items that you are going to report on as deficient is critical. These photos will be included in your home inspection report. One photo per item found is best but sometimes you want to take several pictures of an area of concern to give your client a better idea of the scope of the problem.

When your report template clearly follows your chosen standards of practice the report writing process is easy. This process should be as simple as describing the components that you are required to inspect, listing your inspection findings and attaching photos for these items. If your report writing system is any more complicated than this you should search for another solution.

How you write up an issue is also very important. There is no reason to come across as an overbearing expert or say things in a way that scares your client. Simply state the facts and the location of the deficiency. If you have items to report that are not commonly understood you should state why this finding is important. It is also nice to do your best on explaining why something is happening. Providing this information will help the client better understand why things are happening in the home. A sample B-Sure Inspections report is located in the appendix.

Distributing the Home Inspection Report

Once you have completed the home inspection report it is time to send it to your client. People expect to receive their report in a timely manner. A turnaround of 24 hours should be the maximum timeline for your business. I believe that delivering the home inspection report the same day or evening of the inspection is very important for you and your client. The client and agent want to review the report as soon as possible so that a repair addendum can created and sent to the seller. If you send it the same day or the same evening of the inspection, they can review your report and create the repair addendum in a timely manner.

Getting the report out the same day also benefits the inspector as well. The biggest benefit is that the experience of being in the home is still fresh on your mind. Before you get caught up in the whirlwind of other business or personal activities it is best to just get the report finished. If you wait until the next day you take away the opportunity to inspect another property or perform your routine marketing activities. Also, a new day can bring new distractions or interruptions that may keep you from getting the report done. When this happens your stress level rises because you know people are waiting for the report so that they can get on with their urgent activities.

The report delivery process should be easy and automated. The same system that handles your appointment scheduling should also take care of the report delivery. This system should send an email to your client either with an attachment or a link to download the report. You should also be able to track when the report delivery email was opened by your client. There should also be options to deliver the report directly to the real estate agent representing the buyer. The buyer's agents in my market expect to receive a copy of the home inspection report so that they can walk their client through it. We have a sentence in the inspection agreement that notifies our clients that their agent will also receive a copy of the report. On a rare occasion we will have a client request that we do not send a copy to their agent.

Handling Customer Complaints

Every once and a while you may have an unhappy client or real estate agent. The secret to minimize the chance of having unsatisfied people is to set the proper expectations about the inspection process in advance. The inspection agreement should clearly spell out what standards of practice you follow. It should also clearly state that there are no guarantees that you will find everything. The agreement should also state that there is no warranty and explain what your limits of liability are in plain English. It is also a best practice to send the inspection agreement to your client the day the inspection is booked. This way they have a chance to read and approve it ahead of time. If there is something in the agreement that they question they have chance to get clarification from you in advance.

The day may come when you get an email or a phone call from an unhappy client. If you receive an email you have the advantage of reviewing the inspection report and some time to decide how to respond. Clients that send an email are usually dissatisfied and just appreciate some type of response. On the other hand, when a client calls you, they are usually upset and want some relief immediately. The most important thing to do is to listen to what your client is saying. They need to vent and want to be heard. By letting them talk this gives you some time to prepare your initial response.

Once you have listened to your client's complaint you need to respond appropriately. If your inspection agreement is solid and you have limited your liability you can remind the client about the terms of the signed agreement. Remind them that your ability to root out all the potential problems with a home are limited to a visual inspection of readily accessible areas of the home. Make sure that you follow the terms of the agreement yourself. If your inspection agreement offers to refund the inspection fee only do so if you fail to follow the standards of practice referenced in your agreement. Of course, individual state laws my trump your ability to limit your liabilities. Make sure to consult with an attorney when drafting your inspection agreement to be sure it complies with the laws in your area. A sample inspection agreement is located in the appendix.

Multi-Inspector Firm

Seek first to launch, grow and make money as a single inspector firm. Once you have proven yourself as an expert in your market consider the possibility of hiring additional inspectors. I recommend that you operate your home inspection business for at least three years before hiring your first inspector. Once you become an employer the dynamics of your business changes dramatically. You must now deal with payroll taxes, unemployment taxes, workman's compensation insurance, payroll expenses to name a few.

One big decision that you will face is how much to pay your inspectors. If it is a split of the inspection fee what percentage of the fee should the inspector earn? Do you pay a new inspector 45%, 50% or 55%? What about an experienced inspector? Make sure that you look at all of the costs associated with having employees before you commit to a higher split of the inspection fee.

So, Are You Ready?

The purpose of this book was to give you realistic expectations on what it takes to be a successful home inspector. We have covered all the bases on what you need to do to launch, grow and make money inspecting residential properties. The specific action plans on how to implement each of these steps is something you need to experience for yourself. Another option is to buy a franchise system that shows you exactly how to do.

Nearly eighty percent of new businesses fail within three years of opening. I believe that the failure rate for home inspectors is even higher. The reason I feel this way is that most home inspectors get in to this business because they truly believe that they would be a good inspector. It is true that you need the technical competence to know what you are looking for. What most inspectors fail to realize is that without a solid marketing and operational system there is nothing to inspect. A proven and systematic marketing strategy is the key to any home inspector's long term success. The details on how to specifically implement the successful home inspection marketing strategies outlined in this book are reserved for our B-Sure Inspections franchise owners. Please visit www.yourhomeinspectionfranchise.com to learn more about our home inspection marketing and operational systems for success program. Good luck and welcome to the home inspection industry!

To your unlimited success,

Kirk Bingenheimer

About the Author

After receiving his Bachelor's degree from Michigan State University, Kirk Bingenheimer started his career in residential construction working on a custom home builder's framing crew. A year later he enrolled in the Building Science and Management program at Clemson University where he later earned his Master's degree.

Kirk was a Professor in the Construction Science and Management program at Clemson University in the early 1990's. He became a licensed residential builder in 1994 and spent the next 15 years in pre-construction management positions with some of the nation's largest home builders.

During the housing downturn Kirk launched a new home inspection service in the Charleston, SC market. By end of the third year in business his company was inspecting more than 400 inspections annually. Kirk learned the hard way how to launch, grow and make money inspecting residential properties and he enjoys helping other eager entrepreneurs do the same.

About the Author

Acknowledgments

- The bee characters were purchased from Toons4Biz in June of 2009.
- Any and all marks contained in this book are the property of their respective companies.

Appendix

Sample Inspection Agreement

B-Sure Inspections LLC
LIMITED VISUAL INSPECTION AGREEMENT

THIS AGREEMENT IS SUBJECT TO ARBITRATION PURSUANT TO THE SOUTH CAROLINA UNIFORM ARBITRATION ACT

Property Address: _____ Inspection Fee: _____

This Inspection Agreement contains the terms and conditions of your (the Client) contract with B-Sure Inspections LLC (the Company) for an Inspection of the Property at the above address. This Inspection Agreement contains limitations on the scope of the Inspection and liability. By signing below, Client warrants they will read the entire Inspection Report when received.

1. INSPECTION AND DUTIES
The Company agrees to perform a limited visual Inspection of the systems and components included in the inspection as they exist at the time of the inspection and for which the Client agrees to pay a fee. The Inspection will be performed in accordance with the Standards of Practice (SOP) of the American Society of Home Inspectors

(www.ashi.org), and is limited by the limitations, exceptions and exclusions so stated in the SOP and this Agreement.

2. DISCLAIMER OF WARRANTY

Client understands that the Inspection and Inspection Report do not, in any way, constitute a/an: guarantee, warranty of merchantability or fitness for a particular purpose, express or implied warranty, or insurance policy.

3. NOTICE AND STATUTE OF LIMITATIONS

Client agrees that the inspection is a limited visual inspection of the property and that not all problems with the home may be uncovered. Client also agrees that neither the inspector nor the inspection company has any liability for problems that were not included in the home inspection report.

4. LIMITED LIABILITY CLAUSE

If we fail to perform the Services per the SOP our liability for any and all claims related thereto is limited to the fee paid for the Services, and you release us from any and all additional liability. You understand that the performance of the Services without this limitation of liability would be more technically exhaustive, likely require specialties and would cost substantially more than the fee paid for this limited visual inspection. You understand that you are free to contract with another inspection professional if you do not agree to this provision.

5. ENVIRONMENTAL AND HEALTH ISSUES

The Client specifically acknowledges that a Property Inspection is NOT an Environmental Survey and is not intended to detect, identify, disclose or report on the presence of any actual or potential environmental concerns or hazards in the air, water, soil or building materials. You agree to hold the Company and Inspector harmless for any injury, health risk or damage caused or contributed to by these conditions.

6. LIMITATIONS, EXCEPTIONS AND EXCLUSIONS

The Inspection only includes those systems and components expressly and specifically identified in the Inspection Report. In addition, any area which is not exposed to view, is concealed, is inaccessible because of soil, walls, floors, carpets, ceilings, insulation, and furnishing or in any other fashion is excluded. The Inspection does not include any destructive testing or dismantling.

7. GOVERNING LAW & SERERABILITY

This Agreement shall be governed by South Carolina law.

8. DELIVERY OF REPORT

The client agrees that a copy of the home inspection report will also be shared with their real estate agent.

9. ENTIRE AGREEMENT, MODIFICATION & 3rd PARTIES

This Agreement represents the entire agreement between the parties. No oral agreements, understandings or representations shall change, modify or amend any part of this Agreement. This Agreement shall be binding upon and inure to the parties hereto and their spouses, heirs, executors, administrators, successors, assigns and representatives of any kind whatsoever.

10. DISPUTE RESOLUTION - ARBITRATION CLAUSE

Any dispute, controversy, interpretation related to this contract shall be submitted first to a Non-Binding Mediation conference and absent a voluntary settlement through Non-Binding Mediation to be followed by final and Binding Arbitration, if necessary. Each party to the dispute shall be responsible for their own costs for the arbitration process. The dispute shall be submitted to a sole arbitrator who is knowledgeable and familiar with the professional home inspection industry. If the dispute is submitted to Binding Arbitration, the decision of the Arbitrator appointed there under shall be final and binding and the enforcement of the Arbitration Award may be entered in any Court or administrative tribunal having jurisdiction thereof.

I have read, understand and agree to all the terms and conditions of this Agreement and to pay the fee shown above. Payment for inspection services constitutes acceptance of the Visual Inspection Agreement by Client.

Date: _____

Signature of Client   _____
(One signature binds all)

Printed Name _____

Sample Inspection Report

Summary

This Summary outlines observations found during the visual inspection of the property and cannot be considered a substitute for reading the entire report. Note: The HVAC system was only operated in the heating or cooling mode depending on recent outdoor temperatures.

1. The trees at the corners of the home should be trimmed back to avoid damaged to the shingles.
2. The crawl space door on the left side of the home is bent.
3. There is an active roof leak on the rear of the home above the breakfast nook.
4. There is/has been a roof leak above the dining room. The roof sheathing in the attic has moisture stains that were dry at the time of the inspection.
5. The toilet in the FROG bathroom appears to be leaking at the wax seal. There are moisture stains in the grout and elevated moisture readings at the base of the toilet.
6. The tub spout in the FROG bathroom does not divert all of the water to the shower head.
7. The diverter knob at the front bathroom shower is loose.
8. The floor of the front bathroom shower is flat and water does not drain out rapidly.
9. The tub spout in the rear bathroom does not divert all of the water to the shower head.
10. There are fine cracks in the grout along the perimeter of the master shower.
11. The hot / cold is reversed at the master bathroom garden tub.
12. The hot water tank is approaching the end of its life expectancy.

13. One of the electrical service disconnect boxes on the right side of the home will not open.

14. The plastic protective panel is missing inside the HVAC electrical disconnect boxes in the attic.

15. The smoke detector in the front bedroom is missing.

16. One of the front porch GFCI electrical outlets does not trip when tested.

17. One of the living room ceiling lights is inoperative – likely burned out.

18. The remote for the living room ceiling fan is inoperative – the battery is missing/dead.

19. Three of the kitchen ceiling lights are inoperative – most likely burned out.

20. One of the pendent lights is burned out.

21. The smoke detector in the master bedroom is missing.

22. There is a light switch at the rear wall of the master that likely controls the flood lights.

23. One of the ceiling lights in the master is inoperative – likely burned out.

24. The ceiling fan in the master could not be turned on/off because the batteries for the remote control are missing or dead.

25. The fluorescent light in the master closet is flickering.

26. There are a couple loose electrical outlets in the garage.

27. The flood lights at the rear of the home are inoperative – must likely burned out.

28. There is a little rust on one of the HVAC registers in the FROG. This is likely from cool air leaking out at the metal boot on the attic side and condensation then drips onto the register.

29. There is some dirty insulation in one of the FROG registers. There is likely a tear somewhere inside the flex duct.

30. The HVAC return air filters are dirty.

31. The toilet / shower part of the rear bathroom does not have a HVAC supply register / duct.
32. Some of the insulation for the refrigerant line next to the Heil condenser unit is missing.
33. There are moisture stains under the Heil condensate drain lines in the attic. Insulating these pipes will help prevent the pipes from sweating during the cooling season.
34. The lock for the attic access door in the FROG bathroom is loose.
35. A door knob is missing on one of the FROG attic access doors.
36. One of the closet doors in the front bedroom does not latch properly.
37. The cabinet under the rear bathroom sink is damaged from a previous leak. This area was dry at the time of the inspection.
38. The rear bathroom door knob is loose.
39. One of the rear bedroom closet doors does not latch properly.
40. There was a crack in the drywall at the rear bedroom window that no longer has a gap. This is in the area where the footings were shored up by Mount Valley Foundation Services.
41. The drywall and crown molding in the dining room trey ceiling shows evidence of moisture intrusion. This are lines up closely with the roof leak above. This area was dry at the time of the inspection.
42. The front door should not have a keyed deadbolt on the interior side.
43. One of the French doors to the sunroom does not latch properly.
44. When the front left cooktop burner is on the starter keeps clicking.
45. The right rear knob for the cooktop will not turn.

46. The hardwood flooring in the pantry is cupping from a prior leak. Apparently the ice maker hose was leaking.

47. There are moisture stains in the cabinet below the kitchen sink. This area was dry at the time of the inspection.

48. The drain stopper at one of the master bathroom sinks is stuck in the closed position.

49. There is a small moisture stain on the master bathroom ceiling. This lights up closely with the HVAC condensate lines and supply duct about. This area was dry at the time of the inspection. Monitor during the cooling season.

50. There is an opening between the kitchen and master bedroom behind the refrigerator. This was likely done to give the refrigerator motor a way to cool off.

51. The top sash of one garage window will not close all the way because mud daubers have nested between the frame and sash.

52. The garage doors do not revers when they hit an object.

53. There is a moisture stain on the garage ceiling above the shelves that lines up with the roof leak above. This area was dry at the time of the inspection.

54. There is a moisture stain on the garage ceiling along the edge of the FROG stairway. This area was slightly damp at the time of the inspection. This is likely from the toilet leaking at the wax seal in the FROG bathroom above.

55. Some of the wall insulation in the two story foyer is loose/fallen down.

56. There is some surface fungus on the floor joists in various locations of the crawl space. Installing a higher quality moisture barrier and increasing the ventilation (foundation vent fans) in the crawl space should minimize the fungus activity.

57. There are some rodent droppings in various locations of the crawl space.

58. Some of the crawl space floor insulation is loose or fallen down in a couple locations.
59. The fireplace pilot light works but the flame does not distribute to the logs when turned on.

Site Information

Weather: Cloudy

Ground: Wet

Temperature: 60 degrees

Attendees: Buyer, buyer's agent

Access provided by: Buyer's agent

Occupancy: Home was vacant

Water: On

Electricity: On

Natural Gas: On

Propane Gas: N/A

Approx. start time: 9:00 AM

Approx. End time: 12:30 PM

Approx. age of home: 10 - 15 years

Approx. size of home: 3,500 to 4,000 sqft

Building type: Detached single family

Number of stories: One and one half

Foundation type: Crawl space

Garage, carport: Attached

Structural

Component Descriptions

Foundation: Masonry block piers

Floor structure: Wood joists

Subflooring: OSB

Wall structure: Wood frame - not visible

Ceiling structure: Wood joists, wood trusses

Roof structure: Wood rafters, wood trusses

Roof sheathing: OSB

Observations / Recommendations

  ➢ None

Methods used to inspect under-floor crawl spaces and attics

Crawl space: Entered - access, visibility limited

Attic: Entered - access, visibility limited

Knee wall space: Entered - access, visibility limited

Limitations

Inspection limited / prevented by: Wall, floor and ceiling coverings

The inspector is not required to:

  • Provide engineering or architectural services or analysis

  • Offer an opinion about the adequacy of structural systems and components

  • Enter under-floor crawl space areas that have less than 24 inches of vertical clearance between components and the ground or that have an access opening smaller than 16 inches by 24 inches

Exterior

Component Descriptions
Wall coverings: Brick, cement siding
Flashing: Not visible
Trim: Wood
Paint condition: Good
Exterior doors: Fiberglass, metal
Storm doors: N/A
Storm windows: N/A
Window screens: Present
Decks: N/A
Balconies: N/A
Stoops: Brick
Steps: Brick
Porches: Brick
Railings: Iron
Eaves, soffits, fascia: Aluminum, vinyl
Vegetation: Grass, shrubs, trees
Grading: Sloped away from home
Surface drainage: Storm drains, surface run off
Retaining walls: N/A
Walkways: Brick
Patios: Brick
Driveways: Brick

Observations / Recommendations
- ➢ The trees at the corners of the home should be trimmed back to avoid damaged to the shingles.
- ➢ The crawl space door on the left side of the home is bent.

Limitations

Inspection limited / prevented by: Shrubs against home

Exterior inspected from: Ground level

The inspector is not required to inspect:

- Screening, shutters, awnings, and similar seasonal accessories
- Fences, boundary walls, and similar structures
- Geological and soil conditions
- Recreational facilities
- Outbuildings other than garages and carports
- Seawalls, break-walls and docks
- Erosion control and earth stabilization measures

Photos

Roofing

Component Descriptions
Roof style: Gable, hip
Sloped roofing materials: Asphalt shingles
Flat roofing materials: N/A
Roof drainage systems: Aluminum gutters
Skylights: N/A
Chimneys: N/A
Roof penetrations: Plumbing vent pipes
Probability of leakage: Medium

Observations / Recommendations
➤ There is an active roof leak on the rear of the home above the breakfast nook.
➤ There is/has been a roof leak above the dining room. The roof sheathing in the attic has moisture stains that were dry at the time of the inspection.

Limitations
Methods used to inspect roofing: From the ground, attic space
The inspector is not required to inspect:

- Antennae
- Interiors of vent systems, flues and chimneys that are not readily accessible
- Other installed accessories

Photos

Plumbing

Component Descriptions
Location of main water shut-off: Meter
Interior water supply distribution: PEX
Interior drain, waste, and vent systems: PVC
Sewage ejectors: N/A
Sump pumps: N/A
Natural gas meter: Present
Propane tank: N/A

Water Heating System(s)		
Type:	Conventional tank	
Serves:	Whole house	
Energy sources:	Natural gas	
Energy sources shut-off:	Valve next to heater	
Fuel storage:	N/A	
Fuel distribution:	Steel piping, corrugated stainless steel	
Pressure relief valve:	Present	
Manufacture:	A.O. Smith	
Model number:	FDV50216	
Serial number:	MF02-1744399-216	
Tank capacity:	50 gallons	
Approximate age:	12 years	
Typical life expectancy:	8 to 12 years	
Failure probability:	High	

Observations / Recommendations

➤ The toilet in the FROG bathroom appears to be leaking at the wax seal. There are moisture stains in the grout and elevated moisture readings at the base of the toilet.

➤ The tub spout in the FROG bathroom does not divert all of the water to the shower head.

➤ The diverter knob at the front bathroom shower is loose.

➤ The floor of the front bathroom shower is flat and water does not drain out rapidly.

➤ The tub spout in the rear bathroom does not divert all of the water to the shower head.

➤ There are fine cracks in the grout along the perimeter of the master shower.

➤ The hot / cold is reversed at the master bathroom garden tub.

➤ The hot water tank is approaching the end of its life expectancy.

Limitations

Inspection limited / prevented by: Wall, floor, ceiling covers, insulation

Utilities: N/A

The inspector is not required to inspect:

• Clothes washing machine connections

• Interiors of vent systems, flues, and chimneys that are not readily accessible

• Wells, well pumps, and water storage related equipment

• Water conditioning systems

• Solar, geothermal, and other renewable energy water heating systems

• Manual and automatic fire extinguishing and sprinkler systems

• Landscape irrigation systems

- Septic and other sewage disposal systems
- Determine whether water supply and sewage disposal are public or private
- Determine water quality
- Determine the adequacy of combustion air components
- Measure water supply flow and pressure, and well water quality.
- Fill shower pans and fixtures to test for leaks.

Photos

Electrical

Component Descriptions

Service drop: Overhead - cable type not determined

Amperage rating of the service: 400 Amps

Service entrance conductors: Copper non-metallic sheathed

Service grounding: Ground rod(s) connection not visible

Service main disconnect location: Exterior wall

Distribution panel amperage: 300 Amps (one 200 Amp and one 100 panel)

Distribution panel manufacture: Cutler Hammer

Overcurrent protection devices: Circuit breakers

Branch circuit conductors: Copper non-metallic sheathed

Ground fault circuit interrupters (GFCI): Exterior, garage, bathroom, kitchen

Arc fault circuit interrupters: None found

Smoke alarms: Present

Carbon monoxide alarms: None noted

Observations / Recommendations

➤ One of the electrical service disconnect boxes on the right side of the home will not open.

➤ The plastic protective panel is missing inside the HVAC electrical disconnect boxes in the attic.

➤ The smoke detector in the front bedroom is missing.

➤ One of the front porch GFCI electrical outlets does not trip when tested.

➤ One of the living room ceiling lights is inoperative – likely burned out.

➤ The remote for the living room ceiling fan is inoperative – the battery is missing/dead.

➢ Three of the kitchen ceiling lights are inoperative – most likely burned out.

➢ One of the pendent lights is burned out.

➢ The smoke detector in the master bedroom is missing.

➢ There is a light switch at the rear wall of the master that likely controls the flood lights.

➢ One of the ceiling lights in the master is inoperative – likely burned out.

➢ The ceiling fan in the master could not be turned on/off because the batteries for the remote control are missing or dead.

➢ The fluorescent light in the master closet is flickering.

➢ There are a couple loose electrical outlets in the garage.

➢ The flood lights at the rear of the home are inoperative – must likely burned out.

Limitations

Inspection limited / prevented by: Wall, floor, ceiling covers, insulation

Distribution panel cover: N/A

Utilities: N/A

The inspector is not required to inspect:

- All installed light fixtures, switches and receptacles/outlets
- Remote control devices
- Test smoke and carbon monoxide alarms, security systems, and other signaling and warning devices
- Low voltage wiring systems and components
- Ancillary wiring systems and components not a part of the primary electrical power distribution system
- Solar, geothermal, wind, and other renewable energy systems
- Measure amperage, voltage, and impedance

- Determine the age and type of smoke alarms and carbon monoxide alarms

Photos

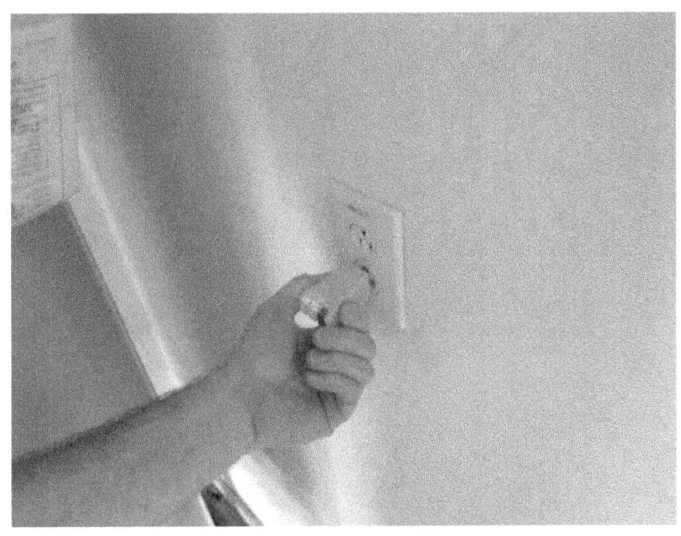

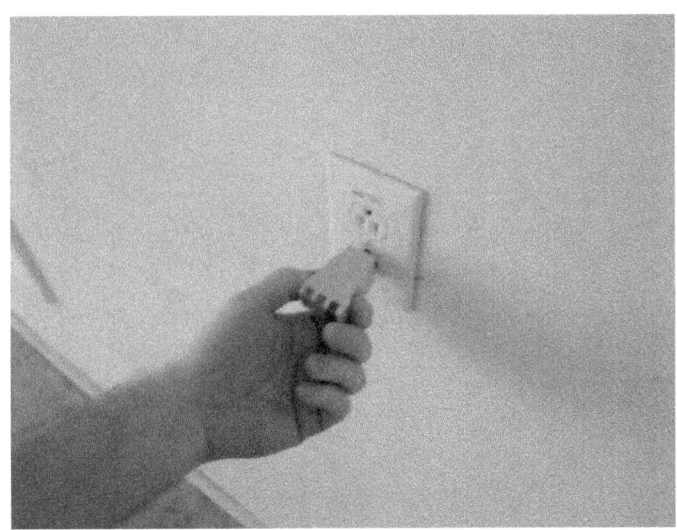

Heating

Component Descriptions

HVAC Heating System(s)		
System type:	Heat pump	Heat pump
Serves:	Sunroom, kitchen, master, FROG	Living, dining, foyer, bedrooms
System location:	Exterior, attic	Exterior, attic
Approximate BTU rating:	N/A	N/A
Filters:	Present	Present
Manufacture:	Heil	Amana
Model number:	H4H348GKE100	RHE24A2D
Serial number:	E120408543	0205100662
Approximate age:	2 years	12 years
Typical life expectancy:	Heat pump - 10 to 15 years	Heat pump - 10 to 15 years
Failure probability:	Low	Medium
Average supply temp:	85 degrees	85 degrees
Average return temp:	65 degrees	70 degrees
Energy source(s)	Electricity	Electricity
Main fuel shutoff:	Electrical distribution panel	Electrical distribution panel
Vent systems, flues, chimney:	N/A	N/A
Heat distribution:	Ducts, registers	Ducts, registers

Observations / Recommendations

➤ There is a little rust on one of the HVAC registers in the FROG. This is likely from cool air leaking out at the metal boot on the attic side and condensation then drips onto the register.

➤ There is some dirty insulation in one of the FROG registers. There is likely a tear somewhere inside the flex duct.

➤ The HVAC return air filters are dirty.

➤ The toilet / shower part of the rear bathroom does not have a HVAC supply register / duct.

Limitations

Inspection limited / prevented by: Wall, floor, ceiling covers, insulation

Warm weather: N/A

Utilities: N/A

The inspector is not required to inspect:

• Interiors of vent systems, flues, and chimneys that are not readily accessible

• Heat exchangers

• Humidifiers and dehumidifiers

• Electrical air cleaning and sanitizing devices

• Solar, geothermal, and other renewable energy heating systems

• Heat-recovery and similar whole-house mechanical ventilation systems

• Determine heat supply adequacy and distribution balance

• Determine the adequacy of combustion air components

Photos

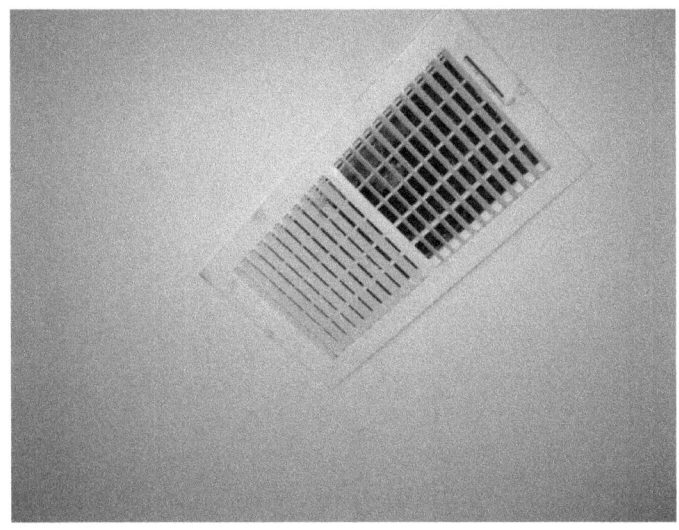

Cooling

Component Descriptions

HVAC Cooling System(s)		
System type:	Heat pump	Heat pump
Serves:	Sunroom, kitchen, master, FROG	Living, dining, foyer, bedrooms
System location:	Exterior, attic	Exterior, attic
BTU rating:	N/A	N/A
Filters:	Present	Present
Manufacture:	Heil	Amana
Model number:	H4H348GKE100	RHE24A2D
Serial number:	E120408543	0205100662
Approximate age:	2 years	12 years
Typical life expectancy:	Heat pump - 10 to 15 years	Heat pump - 10 to 15 years
Failure probability:	Low	Medium
Average supply temp:	N/A - tested in heating mode	N/A - tested in heating mode
Average return temp:	N/A - tested in heating mode	N/A - tested in heating mode
Temperature difference:	N/A	N/A
Acceptable temp difference:	N/A	N/A
Energy source(s)	Electricity	Electricity
Main fuel shutoff:	Electrical distribution panel	Electrical distribution panel

Observations / Recommendations

➤ Some of the insulation for the refrigerant line next to the Heil condenser unit is missing.

➤ There are moisture stains under the Heil condensate drain lines in the attic. Insulating these pipes will help prevent the pipes from sweating during the cooling season.

Limitations

Inspection limited / prevented by: Wall, floor, ceiling covers, insulation

Cool weather: Prevented operation in cooling mode

Utilities: Choose an item.

The inspector is not required to inspect:

- Inspect electric air cleaning and sanitizing devices
- Determine cooling supply adequacy and distribution balance
- Inspect cooling units that are not permanently installed or that are installed in windows

Photos

Interiors

Component Descriptions

Walls: Drywall

Ceilings: Drywall

Floors: Carpet, tile, wood

Steps: Carpet

Stairway railing: Wood

Kitchen counters: Granite

Bath counters: Cultured marble

Cabinets: Wood

Doors: Wood

Windows: Wood

Glazing: Double pane

Garage door(s): Metal

Garage door opener(s): Automatic

Elevator: N/A

Oven: Electric, operational

Range/cooktop: Gas, operational

Range hood: Operational

Microwave: Operational

Dishwasher: Operational

Waste disposal: Operational

Refrigerator: Operational

Observations / Recommendations

- ➢ The lock for the attic access door in the FROG bathroom is loose.
- ➢ A door knob is missing on one of the FROG attic access doors.
- ➢ One of the closet doors in the front bedroom does not latch properly.

- The cabinet under the rear bathroom sink is damaged from a previous leak. This area was dry at the time of the inspection.
- The rear bathroom door knob is loose.
- One of the rear bedroom closet doors does not latch properly.
- There was a crack in the drywall at the rear bedroom window that no longer has a gap. This is in the area where the footings were shored up by Mount Valley Foundation Services.
- The drywall and crown molding in the dining room trey ceiling shows evidence of moisture intrusion. This are lines up closely with the roof leak above. This area was dry at the time of the inspection.
- The front door should not have a keyed deadbolt on the interior side.
- One of the French doors to the sunroom does not latch properly.
- When the front left cooktop burner is on the starter keeps clicking.
- The right rear knob for the cooktop will not turn.
- The hardwood flooring in the pantry is cupping from a prior leak. Apparently the ice maker hose was leaking.
- There are moisture stains in the cabinet below the kitchen sink. This area was dry at the time of the inspection.
- The drain stopper at one of the master bathroom sinks is stuck in the closed position.
- There is a small moisture stain on the master bathroom ceiling. This lights up closely with the HVAC condensate lines and supply duct about. This area was dry at the time of the inspection. Monitor during the cooling season.
- There is an opening between the kitchen and master bedroom behind the refrigerator. This was likely done to give the refrigerator motor a way to cool off.

➢ The top sash of one garage window will not close all the way because mud daubers have nested between the frame and sash.

➢ The garage doors do not revers when they hit an object.

➢ There is a moisture stain on the garage ceiling above the shelves that lines up with the roof leak above. This area was dry at the time of the inspection.

➢ There is a moisture stain on the garage ceiling along the edge of the FROG stairway. This area was slightly damp at the time of the inspection. This is likely from the toilet leaking at the wax seal in the FROG bathroom above.

Limitations

Inspection limited / prevented by: N/A

The inspector is not required to inspect:

- Inspect all installed cabinets
- Inspect all doors and windows
- Paint, wallpaper, and other finish treatments
- Floor coverings
- Window treatments
- Coatings on and the hermetic seals between panes of window glass
- Central vacuum systems
- Recreational facilities
- Installed and free-standing laundry appliances
- Appliance thermostats including their calibration, adequacy of heating elements, self-cleaning oven cycles, indicator lights, door seals, timers, clocks, timed features, and other specialized features of the appliance
- Operate, or confirm the operation of every control and feature of an inspected appliance

Photos

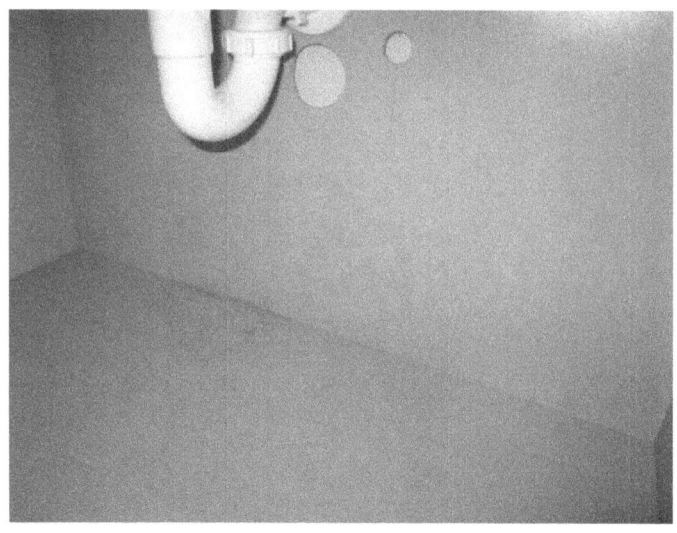

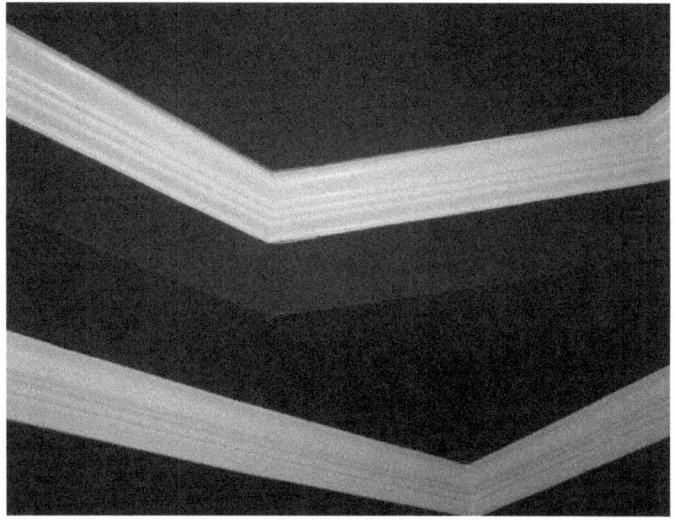

Insulation and Ventilation

Component Descriptions

Attic insulation: Fiberglass

Attic insulation approximate depth: 12 inches

Attic vapor retarders: None found

Attic natural ventilation: Soffit, ridge vents

Attic mechanical ventilation: N/A

Whole house fan: N/A

Kitchen exhaust system: Downdraft to exterior

Bathroom exhaust system: Bath fan(s) vent termination not visible

Laundry room exhaust system: N/A

Clothes dryer exhaust system: Vented to exterior

Crawl space insulation: Fiberglass

Crawl space vapor retarders: Kraft paper

Crawl space moisture barrier type: Plastic

Crawl space moisture barrier coverage: 90%

Crawl space wood moisture content: 15% to 20%

Crawl space natural ventilation: Foundation wall vents

Crawl space mechanical ventilation: N/A

Observations / Recommendations

➢ Some of the wall insulation in the two story foyer is loose/fallen down.

➢ There is some surface fungus on the floor joists in various locations of the crawl space. Installing a higher quality moisture barrier and increasing the ventilation (foundation vent fans) in the crawl space should minimize the fungus activity.

➢ There are some rodent droppings in various locations of the crawl space.

> ➢ Some of the crawl space floor insulation is loose or fallen down in a couple locations.

Limitations

Inspection limited / prevented by: Wall, floor, ceiling coverings
Attic inspection performed: Entered but access, visibility limited
Crawl space inspection performed: Entered but access, visibility limited
Inside of dryer vent duct: Not visible for inspection
The inspector is not required to inspect disturb insulation

Photos

Fireplaces

Component Descriptions
Fireplace type: Prefabricated
Fireplace fuel type: Natural gas
Chimney vent/liner: Non-vented

Observations / Recommendations
➢ The fireplace pilot light works but the flame does not distribute to the logs when turned on.

Limitations
Inspection limited / prevented by: Wall, ceiling coverings
Fireplace fuel sources: N/A
Gas logs: N/A
The inspector is not required to inspect:
- Interiors of vent systems, flues, and chimneys that are not readily accessible
- Fire screens and doors
- Seals and gaskets
- Automatic fuel feed devices
- Mantles and fireplace surrounds
- Combustion air components and to determine their adequacy
- Heat distribution assists (gravity fed and fan assisted)
- Fuel-burning fireplace and appliance located outside the inspected structures
- Determine draft characteristics
- Move fireplace inserts and stoves or firebox contents

Photos

General Limitations and Exclusions

General limitations

A. The inspector is NOT required to perform actions, or to make determinations, or to make recommendations not specifically stated in this Standard.

B. Inspections performed using this Standard:

1. are not technically exhaustive.

2. are not required to identify and to report:

a. concealed conditions, latent defects, consequential damages, and

b. cosmetic imperfections that do not significantly affect a component's performance of its intended function.

C. This Standard applies to buildings with four or fewer dwelling units and their attached and detached garages and carports.

D. This Standard shall not limit or prevent the inspector from meeting state statutes which license professional home inspection and home inspectors.

E. Redundancy in the description of the requirements, limitations, and exclusions regarding the scope of the home inspection is provided for emphasis only.

General exclusions

A. The inspector is NOT required to determine:

1. the condition of systems and components that are not readily accessible.

2. the remaining life expectancy of systems and components.

3. the strength, adequacy, effectiveness, and efficiency of systems and components.

4. the causes of conditions and deficiencies.

5. methods, materials, and costs of corrections.

6. future conditions including but not limited to failure of systems and components.

7. the suitability of the property for specialized uses.

8. compliance of systems and components with past and present requirements and guidelines (codes, regulations, laws, ordinances, specifications, installation and maintenance instructions, use and care guides, etc.).

9. the market value of the property and its marketability.

10. the advisability of purchasing the property.

11. the presence of plants, animals, and other life forms and substances that may be hazardous or harmful to humans including, but not limited to, wood destroying organisms, molds and mold-like substances.

12. the presence of environmental hazards including, but not limited to, allergens, toxins, carcinogens, electromagnetic radiation, noise, radioactive substances, and contaminants in building materials, soil, water, and air.

13. the effectiveness of systems installed and methods used to control or remove suspected hazardous plants, animals, and environmental hazards.

14. operating costs of systems and components.

15. acoustical properties of systems and components.

16. soil conditions relating to geotechnical or hydrologic specialties.

17. whether items, materials, conditions and components are subject to recall, controversy, litigation, product liability, and other adverse claims and conditions.

B. The inspector is NOT required to offer:

1. or to perform acts or services contrary to law or to government regulations.

2. or to perform architectural, engineering, contracting, or surveying services or to confirm or to evaluate such services performed by others.

3. or to perform trades or professional services other than home inspection.

4. warranties or guarantees.

C. The inspector is NOT required to operate:

1. systems and components that are shut down or otherwise inoperable.

2. systems and components that do not respond to normal operating controls.

3. shut-off valves and manual stop valves.

4. automatic safety controls.

D. The inspector is NOT required to enter:

1. areas that will, in the professional judgment of the inspector, likely be dangerous to the inspector or to other persons, or to damage the property or its systems and components.

2. under-floor crawlspaces and attics that are not readily accessible.

E. The inspector is NOT required to inspect:

1. underground items including, but not limited to, underground storage tanks and other underground indications of their presence, whether abandoned or active.

2. items that are not installed.

3. installed decorative items.

4. items in areas that are not entered

5. detached structures other than garages and carports.

6. common elements and common areas in multi-unit housing, such as condominium properties and cooperative housing.

7. every occurrence of multiple similar components.

8. outdoor cooking appliances.

F. The inspector is NOT required to:

1. perform procedures or operations that will, in the professional judgment of the inspector, likely be dangerous to the inspector or to other persons, or to damage the property or its systems or components.

2. describe or report on systems and components that are not included in this Standard and that were not inspected.

3. move personal property, furniture, equipment, plants, soil, snow, ice, and debris.

4. dismantle systems and components, except as explicitly required by this Standard.

5. reset, reprogram, or otherwise adjust devices, systems, and components affected by inspection required by this Standard.

6. ignite or extinguish fires, pilot lights, burners, and other open flames that require manual ignition.

7. probe surfaces that would be damaged or where no deterioration is visible or presumed to exist.

Real Life Testimonials

"As a first time home buyer I was unsure of what to expect, but Scott made the entire process very easy to understand. I feel very confident moving forward with our home buying purchase after our inspection."
Pam – Home Buyer

"From the very beginning, Scott was very professional. He accommodated us at the precise time we desired with a very short notice on my part. The day before the inspection (on a Sunday), he sent us an email reminding us of the appointment and time. His assistant was very polite and helpful.
The whole process was very thorough and the verbal report along with photos was detailed and understandable. If ever I need a home inspection again, Scott will definitely get the job."
Albert – Home Buyer

"Scott was fantastic. He discovered that the house wasn't on a slab as advertised which led us to investigate further. It turns out that the home was illegally built. Scott's inspection saved us thousands of dollars in headaches."
Artie – Home Buyer

"He is the best inspector that we have ever used. Scott was timely with all responses, services and follow up! Very easy to work with, professional, and thorough! Thank you!"
Wendy – Real Estate Agent

"B-Sure inspectors are always professional and on time. Items of concern are explained and photos are provided to assist buyers and sellers with repairs. B-Sure is always at the top of my referral list!"
Patti – Real Estate Agent

"Thanks for your prompt and thorough attention to this home inspection Scott. I appreciate your professionalism."
Herb – Real Estate Agent

Scott was great! Very thorough and took the time to explain his findings to us very clearly. Highly recommend!
Ted – Home Buyer

"Scott is very knowledgeably and helpful. Will call him again!"
Todd – Home Buyer

"Scott was timely with all responses, services and follow up! Very easy to work with, professional, and thorough! Thank you!"
Wendy – Real Estate Agent

"From the very beginning, Scott was very professional. He accommodated us at the precise time we desired with a very short notice on my part. The day before the inspection (on a Sunday), he sent us an email reminding us of the appointment and time. His assistant was very polite and helpful. The whole process was very thorough and the verbal report along with photos was detailed and understandable. If ever I need a home inspection again, Scott will definitely get the job."
Albert – Home Buyer

"Very detailed inspection. We are from out of town and our Realtor recommended you. After reading inspection, we feel confident about the home we're purchasing."

Sherri – Home Buyer

"Hey Scott – I thought you did a great job with the inspection on the house we were looking to purchase -very thorough. We couldn't come to an agreement on repair issues with the sellers, so we will keep looking. Will definitely give you a call. Thanks!"
Scott – Home Buyer

"On time, to the point, handled the buyers well. Thanks for a job well done."
Tamni – Real Estate Agent

"We are out of state, but our real estate agent handled everything. Scott was very prompt and we feel, by looking at his report, that he did an excellent job! He came out pretty quickly after our agent set up the appointment, which we needed done in a timely manner, so we were happy with that also."
Kathi – Home Buyer

"Scott was extremely professional and informative regarding our home inspection. The written report was A-1 and our follow up phone call helped me in making my decisions on our property."
Charles – Home Buyer

"Scott is very knowledgeable and helpful. Will call him again."
Todd – Home Buyer

"Thank you for a great inspection Scott! I would recommend you any day."
Stephanie – Home buyer

"Great job. Complete, detailed and accomplished in a timely manner. Will certainly use and recommend your services.

Jim Oster"

Jim – Real Estate Agent

"Very prompt and professional. Kirk was very thorough."

Bill – Home Buyer

"Scott was very thorough in his inspection and took pictures of all the items he found for my review, and then explained everything to me. This enabled me to be more confident in what I proposed to the seller to have repaired and to feel comfortable in the items I can fix myself. I like that everything is listed and photographed so that I can keep track of everything to make me new home even more perfect!"

Paige – Home Buyer

"The on-line scheduling and payment process was easy to complete and efficient. Email communication and reminders prior to the inspection was very good. The inspector, Kirk was very professional and friendly. He arrived for the inspection on time (he was actually about 10 minutes early). When the inspection was complete he reviewed his findings and walked us through his concerns. He pointed out each concern and documented it in pictures and writing in the report. We received the report via email the next day as promised with a copy to our realtor. We are very satisfied."

Bob – Home Buyer

"Scott was great! Very thorough and took the time to explain his findings to us very clearly. Highly recommend!"

Ted – Home Buyer

"Kirk was extremely thorough and detailed. He even took extra photos based on a suggestion from a friend who is an inspector."
Mary Sue – Home Buyer

"Scott was fast and thorough."
Stanley – Home Buyer

"Kirk could not have possibly been more helpful to us in purchasing our home. He inspected it and then re inspected it and we feel perfectly comfortable with his opinions and recommendations. It has been a much easier process with him in the equation. He is professional, prompt, knowledgeable and proficient."
Anne – Home Buyer

"Kirk scheduled our appointment for a Friday afternoon at 5:00 PM and arrived promptly on time and we were very appreciative for him to schedule it for so late on Friday."
Buddy – Home Buyer

"Excellent. Scott was very professional and thorough. He was enthusiastic and knowledgeable."
Kielo – Home Buyer

"Scott was so thorough when he did the inspection on the home I was selling, that I called him to do the inspection on the home I am buying!"
Ellen – Home Buyer

"Scott was prompt, thorough, and professional in every way during the course of my buyer's home inspection. The best part of the service is that we received our completed report just hours after the inspection was through."

John – Real Estate Agent

"Kirk came on short notice from our agent. He was prompt, polite and professional. I was on sight along with our agent and he took the time to walk us through any issues and thoroughly explain them and what needed to be done to resolve them. I have since called him to request a re inspection of the issues once repaired and have full confidence in his assessment of the property."
Anne – Home Buyer

"This is my second home that ya'll have inspected for me and I wouldn't trust anyone else! I am also excited about checking out your concierge service this time as I can use all the help I can get! Thanks!"
Deanne – Home Buyer

"Thanks for being so efficient!!"
David – Home Buyer

"Very professionally and thoroughly conducted inspection. Everything well covered in the report and in the presentation made by the inspector directly at the property. The inspector didn't rush it and gave plenty of time for questions."
Gunnar – Home Buyer

"We asked numerous questions and received detailed answers which have proved useful in evaluating the house as well as making future repairs. Scott possesses a great deal of technical information and he was able to respond in a detailed way which we found most helpful. We appreciated his honesty and directness as well as his wealth of technical knowledge."
Michael – Home Buyer

"Kirk's report was very thorough and comprehensive. And he was more than willing to speak with us to answer questions we had about the written report. Having the benefit of his experience and insights was hugely helpful. A++ for his customer service. Many thanks!"

Frank – Home Buyer

"When our heat pump stopped working, it made more sense to me to have a professional who doesn't sell HVAC tell me exactly what we were facing. I had several other questions as well. Kirk came on short notice, inspected and answered every question with photos to illustrate his findings and recommendations, and we his written recommendations within just a few hours. That helped me proceed with confidence as I interviewed companies about repair or replacement of our heating and air conditioning system. I would use Kirk again and highly recommend him."

John – Home Owner

"B-Sure is a very professional company with First Class employees that are very knowledgeable and experienced. We would not hesitate to recommend this company too anyone that has a need for a home inspection."

Bill – Home Buyer

"Quick response to meeting new home buy schedule, very detailed, excellent report, courteous and helpful."

Lee – Home Buyer

"Kirk presented us with an amazingly detailed and comprehensive report after spending hours going through the home with our realtor. His findings were very informative and we feel lucky to have such a thorough insight. Thankfully the owners are agreeing to take care of

most of the issues. We are truly appreciative of the work Kirk has done and look forward to talking with him soon."
Carolyn – Home Buyer

"I would highly recommend Kirk to anyone in need of this kind of service. He showed up on time, was very professional and did a very thorough job."
Stan – Home Buyer

"I am very pleased with the home inspection that I received. Scott did a terrific job. His report was 40 pages in length and included a detailed description of all items both major and minor as well as pictures to support it. The inspection report alerted me to some major issues that were not visible to me. I would highly recommend Scott and will use him again in the future."
Brian – Home Buyer

"Scott did a great job. He was on time, efficient and professional. Thank you so much."
Bobbi – Home Buyer

"We're not novice home buyers, but we had been looking for quite a while for the 'right' house and were excited when we thought we had found 'it'. We were so excited that we didn't take a lot of time looking at the details of the dwelling before we put in an offer. Our home inspector was thorough and professional home inspection showed us major items that we had missed in our excitement. He kept us from making a HUGE mistake in purchasing that house."
Ed – Home Buyer

"I can always count on B-Sure Inspections to address my clients concerns with the sale or purchase of a home. Our home inspector was

very thorough and explains not only the potential problem but more importantly puts it in a context that the clients and I can understand. The home inspection reports make it easy to read and he is always available for further explanation. I trust him to work with myself and my clients to make the process smooth and reassuring for all parties. I would gladly, and often do, refer him to clients and other real estate professionals."
Danielle. – Real Estate Agent

"Our home inspector was extremely professional and attentive throughout our home inspection process. Even after the report had been completed and delivered, he stayed available and engaged in our issues until they were resolved to his satisfaction. My client was very appreciative and I highly recommend B-Sure Inspections."
David – Real Estate Agent

"Thank you so much for your prompt attention to my client's needs. As you know, these were very "picky" people and I really appreciate the great job you did with not only the home inspection but also the customer service you afforded them. Your calm explanations and your knowledge as a builder really kept the sale together. I'm looking forward to working with our home inspector again in the near future."
Faye – Real Estate Agent

"I found our home inspector to be a true professional. He was courteous, showed attention to detail and always provided his home inspection services in a timely manner. My Buyer was very happy with his services and I would highly recommend him."
Linda – Real Estate Agent

"I was lucky enough to find a home that I really loved, but of course, that doesn't make it the right one. I contacted B-Sure Inspections to

have them come and inspect my new 'dream home'. The turn-around time from phone call to the home inspection was amazing. The home inspection was very thorough. It was not the rush-in and rush-out, thanks for the check. A detailed explanation was provide to me in writing and most importantly to me, I was spoken to in laymen's' terms so that I understood the completeness of the inspection and the concerns that our home inspector had after the inspection. I recommend B-Sure Inspections to anyone who is looking for confirmation on their "dream home."
Beverly – Home Buyer

"I highly recommend Kirk with B-Sure Inspections. Our home inspector was prompt, courteous and very professional home inspection. Most importantly, the home inspection was thorough and my clients were very satisfied!"
Kendall – Real Estate Agent

Was very happy!
Carol – Real Estate Agent

Fantastic Company. Prompt! Very considerate to answer all questions.
Dineen – Real Estate Agent

Arrived on time, explained what he saw to me as WE inspected the property, paused several times during the inspection to go back over items to be sure I understood them and to ensure nothing was missed, explained items in layman's terms, identified items for future maintenance and how to perform the maintenance.
Churchill – Home Buyer

We had further questions about our inspection, and were able to reach Scott the first try. He answered all of our questions and we felt very confident that he did a thorough inspection.

Lucy – Home Buyer

Scott was very thorough and helped me understand every issue I had questions about. As a buyer I was very pleased with the professionalism and thorough handling of the inspection of our potential vacation home. Thanks!

Lynn – Home Buyer

Great experience. I feel Kirk did a thorough inspection, and a wonderful job in explaining all issues of the report. I really appreciate Kirk going above and beyond with my real estate transactions!

George – Home Buyer

Thanks for quick and courteous service! And for wearing booties in the house!

Rebecca – Real Estate Agent

We are moving here from out of state, and were not present for the inspection. Scott performed it and sent us a detailed report within 1 day and was extremely thorough in his process. We are glad we hired you guys!

Michael – Home Buyer

"Scott was wonderful! He was prompt and thorough. He took very detailed photos and descriptions of all the problems. He also provided exact locations of issues, to make it easier for the contractor to fix. Thank you so much!"

Lindsay – Home Buyer

"Very Professional and detail oriented home inspector. Received inspection report in a very timely manner. Would feel comfortable to inquire from Scott references for other services that we may need as new homeowners in South Carolina. Much Appreciative."
Susan – Home Buyer

"Kirk at B-Sure Inspections did a thorough home inspection, they showed up on time and the report was easy to ready!"
Elizabeth – Real Estate Agent

"Kirk always does a great job. I like that he takes the time to answer any questions that my buyers and I might have. I never feel that he is rushing to get to his next inspection."
Jenny – Real Estate Agent

"Scott was very thorough, and detailed. I feel like we got a clear picture of what needed to be addresses. His photos and report were so helpful. Thank you."
Lindsay – Home Buyer

"Scott was very prompt and professional home inspector."
Maria – Real Estate Agent

"I live out of state. So my Realtor and my brother met with Kirk after he finished his inspection. He took the time to answer all their questions and emailed me a very detailed home inspector. Thank you ever so much for being so thorough."
Angi – Home Buyer

"Professional, on time, thorough & conversant, therefore, we had a complete understanding of the property's issues and non-issues."
Suzanne – Home Buyer

"Kirk was tedious, extremely knowledgeable, friendly, professional and passionate about getting things right. I feel extremely confident we got the 'right' home inspector."
Marshall – Home Buyer

"Great experience with Kirk! Thorough home inspector and was detailed with my first time home buyer."
Molly – Real Estate Agent

"Scott was thorough, professional and explained deficits in an understandable way. I was very impressed."
Rose-Mary – Home Buyer

"Scott came on time, did a very intense survey of the town home, and finished on time. He had told me it would take 1/2 hours, and it did. He discussed problems and showed me photos. He was also very pleasant home inspector. This is the second time I've used your services. In 2011 he also inspected two homes, one of which I purchased. Thank you."
Susan – Home Buyer

"Scott did an outstanding job on our recent home inspection request; quick to respond to our needs, timely in arrival on site, timely in his report, conducted a thorough and professional inspection. Could not be more pleased."
Frank– Home Buyer

"Scott did an excellent job and really helped my buyers make an informed decision."
John– Real Estate Agent

"Kirk always does a great job and works well with our clients!"
Keith– Real Estate Agent

"Great doing business with Kirk and B-Sure Inspections. Kirk set aside a time of 9-12 for my client's home inspector. I arrived about 10 minutes early to see Kirk already checking out the property. He was very thorough and took the time to show his pictures and explain his findings. He had the inspection report to my client in less than 2 hours. I would highly recommend him to other clients and agents in the area."
Scott – Real Estate Agent

"Kirk did a great job! He arrived on time and was very professional home inspector. The report was great! Good pictures and descriptions made the report easy to read and understand! Our real estate agent has already suggested B-Sure Inspections to another buyer!"
Cliff – Home Buyer

"Kirk is always prompt and professional. He is great to work with and very accommodating home inspector."
Eric– Real Estate Agent

"Kirk was excellent! I had my inspection last week and was extremely impressed with the service I received. Kirk was early to the appointment and we got started right when he said we would. He was very friendly and did not make me feel like I was bothering him, even though I followed him around for the whole home inspection. He took time to explain everything he saw, and even gave me little pointers about how I might be able to make improvements, which I really liked. He spent about 1.5 to 2 hours on the inspection and final summary with us at the end. I received the inspection report by email on the same day as the inspection, and was happy with the quality of the report. He crawled around in both the attic and the crawlspace for about 15 minutes each, and was obviously not afraid to get dirty / sweaty. I appreciated that I saved $25 dollars by scheduling my appointment online, and that I was able to pay by personal check, cash, or charge at the conclusion of the inspection. I would absolutely recommend Kirk and B-Sure inspections to anyone looking for a professional and thorough home inspector. I will also be adding this review to Angie's List, and will be giving A's for everything"

Alex Green – Home Buyer
"They are very thorough, get the report to you quickly, and the photos are great."
Andrea– Real Estate Agent

"When I shared the home inspection report with the buyer's contractor, he said, "I like this report because it is thorough and the pictures are clear". He said it was the best report. I agree! Scott was very professional home inspector!"
Maria– Real Estate Agent

"Scott did a great job. Very thorough home inspector."
Will – Home Buyer

"Scott was fantastic! Very professional home inspector and took the time to go through and explain everything he found!"
Edward – Home Buyer

"Great job in pointing out problem areas and making some suggestions on how to approach addressing them. Would definitely use then again."
Mark – Home Buyer

"Kirk was incredibly diligent and detailed in his reporting. The final report was sent the same evening as the inspection and it was sent electronically, with very high quality pictures and all. Kirk did a great job. I would recommend this home inspector to anyone who wants to know what they are getting into. Provides a great too to negotiate with a sell as well."
John – Home Buyer

"Was willing and able to schedule home inspector according to the buyer's work schedule. Quick turnaround on providing the inspection report – very thorough and detailed."
Karen – Real Estate Agent

"Wonderful service. Will definitely recommend to others!"
Megan – Home Buyer

"Scott was a pleasure to work with. He was very professional and did a thorough job. He was patient and walked my client through all his findings. I would recommend this home inspector to future clients."
Nichole – Real Estate Agent

"Because of the large amount of anticipated repairs and renovations to the home we were about to purchase for our family, Kirk came to the home twice and made certain that he listed each and every item no matter how small. We now have a complete checklist of everything that our contractor will need to address. We will use B-Sure for all of our business and investment properties going forward!"
Reta – Home Buyer

"Kirk was extremely professional, knowledgeable, prompt and friendly home inspector. I couldn't have asked for a better home inspection experience. I highly recommend B-Sure Inspections."

Jennifer – Home Buyer

"Kirk and staff were very helpful. Even before the home inspection the automated online scheduling service was easy and it saved me $25! The home inspection was thorough and it gave me tons of information on the home I am purchasing. I will definitely use them again."
Jason – Home Buyer

"Scott was great! He was very thorough home inspector, and his findings alerted us to many problems and made sure we didn't get ourselves into a money pit."
Edward– Home Buyer

"Based on the thoroughness of the home inspectors report and photos it is good to see that a buyers interests are captured."
Doug– Home Buyer

I've had two home inspections in the last month on two different properties and Kirk and Scott have done them. I'm extremely pleased with how thorough they have been!
Joe – Home Buyer

"Scott was a great home inspector!"
Walter – Home Buyer

"Again, thank you for your attention to detail on the inspection. Great to have it crossed off the list. I so appreciate it and the way you do business. I will indeed recommend you."
Marilyn – Home Buyer

"We experienced a slight problem when our Realtor had not ensured that the gas was turned on during the home inspection. Scott could easily have charged us again for coming back out when it was turned on but he did not. He was very professional and knowledgeable home inspector. Thanks so much!"

Claire – Home Buyer

"My husband is in the military and currently overseas while I am residing on the west coast until his return in the spring. When he returns, our next tour will be spent in Charleston SC. There is a home we fell in love with but it is sight unseen. As you can imagine Kirk's inspection was more than just an overview of the structure. Kirk was our eyes and ears and his report was incredibly detailed!! He discovered some serious structural issues and though it is not a deal breaker for us we are now better able to approach the negotiating table with a clear understanding of the work that will need to be done. I cannot imagine the nightmare that would have been awaiting us if Kirk hadn't been as thorough and professional as he was! Our appreciation is beyond words! I would HIGHLY recommend Kirk to ANYONE who is in need of a home inspector!!! Thank you SO MUCH Kirk!!! P.S. He was also kind enough to offer a military discount!"

Crystal – Home Buyer

"Kirk went to Columbia from Charleston to inspect my house, as promised, even though his other reason for going up to Columbia fell through. I appreciated his integrity in keeping his promise although it was not to his advantage, a rare quality in this day and time. He was very thorough and caught a couple if issues that I suspect other inspectors may have missed."

Steven – Home Buyer

"Our Realtor suggested B-Sure for the home inspection. I contacted Kirk through their web site and it was fast and easy. Kirk did a great job and answered my questions very promptly. I would refer B-Sure to

my friends and anyone needing a home inspector. Also Kirk's experience played a major role in my decision making with having excellent knowledge of construction/renovation process."
Don – Home Buyer

"At first I was hesitant to have a home inspection done, especially on a new home. My wife insisted that we needed an inspection. I could not be more proud of her or you for the inspection being done. You were professional and thorough and you found things that I would never have thought of. I cannot thank you enough and I will recommend you to everyone who needs a home inspector. Thank you very much"
John – Home Buyer

"B-Sure Inspections did a great job. I would not hesitate to use this inspection service in the future. Our home inspector found at least four items that I missed. I have been in the building industry for over forty years. Thanks for a great home inspection!"
Charles – Home Buyer

"Scott was an excellent resource — he added a personal touch to the home inspection, addressed all our personal concerns, and had expertise to speak knowledgeably about every aspect of the home."
Corey – Home Buyer

"On time, very professional and Kirk took the time to sit down and go over his findings. Received a very detailed report with pictures of all areas of concern within 24 hours. I would use this home inspector again in a heartbeat."
Frank – Home Buyer

"Kirk was very helpful and knowledgeable about everything. Our home inspector has a very friendly attitude throughout the entire home

inspection process. He answered all my questions and got the report back in a very timely manner."
Amanda – Home Buyer

"Scott made things very easy. Scheduling was quick, inspection was thorough, and he provided excellent customer service to my buyer client for our home inspection."
Molly – Real Estate Agent

"Scott Powell was very thorough and very professional home inspector. I was impressed with our home inspection."
Mary – Home Buyer

"My Realtor suggested Kirk as the home inspection professional t use to evaluate this older home that was offered as a bank short sale. Since the sale was without reps and warrants, I truly appreciated his professional review of the home and his straight forward assessment of the home's condition."
Rosa – Home Buyer

"Never equated a home inspection with a great customer experience – but I do now! Kirk was great. He was prompt, professional and extremely helpful. I would not hesitate for a second to use B-Sure Inspections again, and again, and again."
Chris – Home Buyer

"Kirk was very professional and thorough home inspector. My wife and I will definitely use B-Sure Inspections again for our home inspection!"
Chris – Home Buyer

"Once again, a job well done for my client's home inspection."

David – Real Estate Agent

"Kirk was very professional, helpful and informative home inspector."
Brian – Home Buyer

"Many thanks to Scott for making our home inspection an easy process! He was professional, friendly and thorough. Afterwards, he patiently explained all of the issue found in the house."
Jeanne – Home Buyer

"Kirk was on time, professional, and shared all his information before he even left the house. My client loved that. Delivery of the home inspection report was fast. Thanks!"
Kristin – Real Estate Agent

"I met Kirk at our home inspection and he did a great thorough job of inspecting the property. It added a lot of ease of mind with my new purchase."
Chris – Home Buyer

"Our Charleston inspection was on time, clean, courteous and thorough."
Lee – Home Buyer

"Kirk was very reliable and thorough on his home inspection for my client. He was very pleasant to work with."
Michelle – Real Estate Agent

"Kirk was professional, thorough and communicative. This is what I would expect from a home inspection."
Steve – Home Buyer

"I've been recommending a home inspection from B-Sure Inspections to my clients for the last 9 months and they are always timely, professional and knowledgeable."
Amy – Real Estate Agent

"My Realtor recommended B-Sure Inspections, and I couldn't happier with the experience. The report was very specific and laid out what repairs needed to be addressed before the sale. Kirk was exceptionally professional and thorough. I appreciated the ease of scheduling online as well as the online payment option. THANK YOU for making this part of our real estate purchase so easy. I will definitely recommend you to others for their home inspection."
Rebecca – Home Buyer

"Scott is very professional and personable. He took the extra time to go over any concerns, and to point out items that my buyer might need to be aware of. I will definitely use Scott again, and refer him to other clients for their home inspection."
Sharyn – Real Estate Agent

"Thorough and professional in every respect. I would recommend Kirk to anyone needing a home inspection services."
Bill – Home Buyer

"Scott was very helpful. I called him to clarify some items and despite the fact he was on vacation (I did not know when I called), he insisted that he answer my questions. Without my report in front of him he had total recall and was most helpful in his suggestions. I would highly recommend him for your home inspection."
Betty – Home Buyer

"He was on time, did a very detailed home inspection, when over the information and we received the report the next day. I was very pleased and would refer to others."
Debra – Home Buyer

"Scott was very professional home inspection and did an excellent job!"
Katey – Home Buyer

"Very personable, helpful and professional home inspection."
Jennifer – Home Buyer

"Professional home inspection service: low on drama and high on substance!"
Cary – Real Estate Agent

"Your company saved us from making a costly mistake. As a retired Inspector of Buildings for a municipality, I found your inspection to be very informative and complete. We will definitely be using your services again in the near future for our next home inspection."
Rob – Home Buyer

"Scott was extremely professional and detailed. He made the entire home inspection process enjoyable and he answered any question in the inspection we had. We are very grateful for his services."
Greg – Home Buyer

"Kirk was on time, polite to my buyers and gave a thorough home inspection report."
Molly – Real Estate Agent

"Our experience with Scott was great. He was very knowledgeable home inspection and did a very good job. He took the time to explain everything. He was very pleasant to talk too.
Bill – Home Buyer

"Scott helped me from making one of the biggest mistakes of my life. I am very grateful for our home inspection!"
Patty – Home Buyer

"Just wanted to take a minute to thank you again Scott. Bill and I enjoyed speaking with you and the report was very comprehensive. I will definitely pass along your company as the way to go for home inspection!"
Wendy – Home Buyer

"Our home Inspection was on time and prompt. Very Nice. Everything went well and the report looked good!"
Molly – Real Estate Professional

"Thank you for your prompt and professional home inspection service!"
Richard – Real Estate Professional

"We were so pleased with Kirk's Inspection. Not only did he complete it on short notice: he did a great job on the inspection. There were photos, a complete report, and after we received all of it, we called him for some additional help which he willingly provided. We highly recommend B-Sure Inspections for your home inspection.
Marlene – Home Buyer

"I just finished a home inspection for a valued customer that I entrusted to B-Sure Inspections. This was a big sale and I needed a

very accurate picture that the home my buyer was purchasing was as good on the inside as it looked on the outside. Since I used B-Sure Inspections for purchase of my personal residence I was comfortable that I had the right home inspector. The best thing was the report format was easy for me to translate into a very user-friendly repair addendum and I closed the deal very quickly. If you want a company that will work with you and truly listen to your client needs I'd go with B-Sure – without hesitation, I give them my highest endorsement."
Don – Real Estate Agent

"I am quite pleased with the work performed by your company. The scheduling process was quick and easy. The inspections itself was very thorough and professionally done. I will definitely recommend you to anyone needing a home inspection. Thanks for a job well done."
June – Home Buyer

"Once again you went above and beyond what is expected out of a home inspection and answered my client's questions in easy to understand terms making my clients feel comfortable with their purchase. You are a true professional and there is no question I would recommend B-Sure Inspections to anyone needing a home inspection."
Charlie – Real Estate Agent

"Thanks so much for the in-depth and prompt home inspection service. The home inspection report really explained to me in plain English what the positives and negatives of the house were."
 David – Home Buyer

"Kirk did a great job! He came through for my buyers when they needed a home inspection quick. The report was easy to read and very thorough. I will definitely use him again!"
Molly – Real Estate Agent

"Thank you so much for taking the extra time to explain the home inspection to my wife and me. It was a pleasure meeting with you. Having all the documentation sent via email has been very helpful. I will be sure to recommend you to others as your knowledge and professionalism was greatly appreciated."
Brian – Home Buyer

"I cannot thank you enough for going 'beyond the call of duty' and supporting both my buyers and me by taking the time to meet the national builder and their HVAC contractor and standing by your conviction that the new system was not operating properly. Upon re-inspection of the National Builder's HVAC contractor to find as you described that the system was not operating properly. You saved my buyers thousands of dollars, as well as, headaches and frustration. Now they love their new home and they will always remember how you stood strong and were there for 'Them' during the home inspection process of contract to closing."
Janice – Real Estate Agent

"I've been in the Real Estate business for 14 years and have utilized the services of many building inspectors. Kirk Bingenheimer, with B-Sure Inspections, is without a doubt the most thorough, professional home inspection I have ever used. He always meets with the buyer at the end of the inspection to explain any deficiencies he found, and I appreciate the manner in which he discusses these issues with the buyer. I recently met him for an inspection on a newly constructed home. Although told the house would be ready for the inspection, when we arrived, it was not completely finished. He was very understanding and agreeable to do as much of the inspection as he could, and return on another date when the house was finished. I truly appreciated his flexibility! I will continue to recommend Kirk to my buyers!"

Beth – Real Estate Agent

"Kirk at B-Sure Inspections exceeded our expectations. We are extremely pleased with the home inspection, and would definitely use the company again. The report was complete, easy to read and did find a few minor problems with our new home that needed repair. B-Sure Inspections also found a major problem that needed immediate attention before closing."
Gale – Home Buyer

"B-Sure Inspections does an excellent job, thank you so much! This home inspection was thorough, any questions I had at the time were answered, and the report was detailed but also easy to read."
Kyle – Home Buyer

"Your work was impressive and of the highest quality. The summary report was extremely comprehensive and is a huge assistance in the repair of our new home. We have already referred you to some of our friends. Thank you again for all of your help, and I will certainly be in touch with you if I require more of your home inspection services."
Brandon – Home Buyer

"I received my homeowner's inspection report promptly after the home inspection. Not being present at the inspection, I was totally reliant on the thoroughness of the inspection process and was more than satisfied at the precise and detailed review which was also accompanied by photographs of specific issues that had to be addressed. All in all, it was a very professional and complete job. Thank you kindly."
Sonia – Home Buyer

"Recently my daughter used B-Sure Inspections for a home inspection. She wanted me to see the report that was issued, to make sure she understood everything. I was thoroughly impressed with the report because of its quality, detail and clarity. It was first class all the way. I'm now buying a house and yes, B-Sure just completed my inspection also. Again, I was impressed. Kirk made the whole process so easy for me. I highly recommend B-Sure Inspections to anyone wanting a first class job"
Taylor – Home Buyer

"I was immediately impressed by your website and the ease at which I could enter all information, make an appointment, and receive a confirmation almost instantly. Both my client and I thought that your explanations as to the reason from some of the repairs was an excellent feature of your service. The home inspection report was very thorough and contained precise information to be able to have the repairs done correctly."
Laura – Realtor

"Thank you for doing our home inspection. I am very happy with your service. I liked the way you explained everything to us. Your service was very helpful. Again, thanks so much."
Lyman – Home Buyer

"We are very satisfied with the home inspection that you performed for us. From the scheduling of the inspection to the timeliness of the report, we were well pleased. You were easily accessible and answered our questions fully. We appreciated the expertise and knowledge that you shared with us. We will readily recommend your service to others. It has been a pleasure to do business with you."
Mary – Home Buyer

"As a real estate professional and recent home buyer, I know the importance of securing a quality home inspection. After investigating many firms that offer this service, I determined that B-Sure Inspections was the one I needed to ensure my investment. Kirk's expertise gave me confidence that all potential issues had been addressed and I could proceed with the purchase. I especially appreciated the immediate feedback Kirk's inspection process provided. I have personally bought 7 homes over the last 30 years and I rank B-Sure Inspections as the most professional and thorough home inspection service I have ever used. I am happy to give them my strongest endorsement."
Don – Home Buyer

Thanks so much for the excellent home inspection that you performed. Your professionalism, responsiveness, and accommodating approach are greatly appreciated and valued. I will definitely keep your firm in mind should I have any future needs for a home inspection.
Patrick – Home Buyer

"Kirk did an excellent home inspection. He brings a lot of knowledge and experience to his clients. He was very professional when the seller showed up gave us a great overview of what he found before he left."
Jenny – Real Estate Agent

www.ingramcontent.com/pod-product-compliance
Lightning Source LLC
Chambersburg PA
CBHW051513170526
45165CB00002B/458